Poems

Volume II

THE MACMILLAN COMPANY
NEW YORK . BOSTON . CHICAGO . DALLAS
ATLANTA . SAN FRANCISCO

MACMILLAN & CO., Limited
LONDON . BOMBAY . CALCUTTA
MELBOURNE

THE MACMILLAN CO. OF CANADA, Ltd.
TORONTO

Poems

By
John Masefield

Volume II

New York
The Macmillan Company
1925

INTRODUCTION

I have been asked to write a few words as introduction to this volume, which contains four narrative poems.

I wrote Reynard the Fox partly because the events of a fox hunt have been for some centuries the deepest pleasure in English country life, and partly because the fox hunt brings together on terms of equality all sorts and conditions of the English people. I am always sad that this friendship and equality is purchased by the tormenting and possible death of an animal. I wish that it were not so, but huntsmen tell me that hounds will not hunt unless they kill their fox fairly often and that they will not show the same enthusiasm for the red herring soaked in aniseed. Setting aside altogether the question of its cruelty, I felt that a fox hunt made a frame in which many of the more permanent types of English character might be portrayed. The setting and outward appearance of a fox hunt are always most beautiful and its events exciting, though, no doubt, these things have always meant and will always mean more to the English people than to any other.

In the poem about a steeplechase I was concerned mainly with the idea of the subtle relation between horse and rider which in moments of excitement, in the race, the hunt, or even the panic, make them curiously one. I was also interested in the spiritual nature of contests, in which the individual souls of the competitors must be swayed, not only by their own feelings, but by the intensely excited feelings and desires of many thousands of partisans close by. Sometimes, in watching contests at which many thousands of spectators have been present, I have felt that the competing emotions of the partisans almost took spiritual shape and fought above the competitors.

In the poem Enslaved, as in Reynard the Fox, I was concerned with the idea of escape. The story is taken partly from two anecdotes in Burton's "Anatomy of Melancholy" and partly from one of the shorter stories of the "Arabian Nights," mixed with a good deal of matter of my own.

King Cole is in part a tribute to the circus, a form of art most beautiful and moving, which I hope will never perish, though modern forms of amusement have certainly reduced the numbers of circuses on the English roads. Perhaps most people go to circuses solely for the amusement which they give and for the excitement and beauty of the moving horses, but some among these must also have the feeling that the art of the circus is of a reality not common in the art of modern times. It uses the entire being of the artists. I was interested in King Cole, because I lived for some years in what was said to have been his parish. Others have denied that he had anything to do with this particular parish and have given him a greater splendour than our popular nursery rhyme. In any case he must be a shadowy figure. Whenever I pass a little chalk hill in Berkshire, I like to think that the grove of hawthorn and bramble on the top covers the place where King Cole is buried.

Of the little poem, The Dream, printed at the end of this volume, I need only say that it should be read as the record of a dream.

JOHN MASEFIELD.

Oxford, 1925

CONTENTS

REYNARD THE FOX; OR, THE GHOST HEATH RUN

The meet was at "The Cock and Pye
By Charles and Martha Enderby,"
The grey, three-hundred-year-old inn
Long since the haunt of Benjamin
The highwayman, who rode the bay.
The tavern fronts the coaching way,
The mail changed horses there of old.
It has a strip of grassy mould
In front of it, a broad green strip.
A trough, where horses' muzzles dip,
Stands opposite the tavern front,
And there that morning came the hunt,
To fill that quiet width of road
As full of men as Framilode
Is full of sea when tide is in.

The stables were alive with din
From dawn until the time of meeting.
A pad-groom gave a cloth a beating,
Knocking the dust out with a stake.
Two men cleaned stalls with fork and rake,
And one went whistling to the pump,
The handle whined, ker-lump ker-lump,
The water splashed into the pail,
And, as he went, it left a trail,
Lipped over on the yard's bricked paving.
Two grooms (sent on before) were shaving
There in the yard, at glasses propped

On jutting bricks; they scraped and stropped,
And felt their chins and leaned and peered,
A woodland day was what they feared
(As second horsemen), shaving there.
Then, in the stalls where hunters were,
Straw rustled as the horses shifted,
The hayseeds ticked and haystraws drifted
From racks as horses tugged their feed.
Slow gulping sounds of steady greed
Came from each stall, and sometimes stampings,
Whinnies (at well-known steps) and rampings
To see the horse in the next stall.

Outside, the spangled cock did call
To scattering grain that Martha flung.
And many a time a mop was wrung
By Susan ere the floor was clean.
The harness room, that busy scene,
Clinked and chinked from ostlers brightening
Rings and bits with dips of whitening,
Rubbing fox-flecks out of stirrups,
Dumbing buckles of their chirrups
By the touch of oily feathers.
Some, with stag's bones rubbed at leathers,
Brushed at saddle-flaps or hove
Saddle linings to the stove.
Blue smoke from strong tobacco drifted
Out of the yard, the passers snifft it,
Mixed with the strong ammonia flavor
Of horses' stables and the savour
Of saddle-paste and polish spirit
Which put the gleam on flap and tirrit.
The grooms in shirts with rolled-up sleeves,
Belted by girths of coloured weaves,
Groomed the clipped hunters in their stalls.

One said "My dad cured saddle galls,
He called it Doctor Barton's cure;
Hog's lard and borax, laid on pure."
And others said, "Ge' back, my son,"
"Stand over, girl; now, girl, ha' done."
"Now, boy, no snapping; gently.   Crikes
He gives a rare pinch when he likes."
"Drawn blood? I thought he looked a biter."
"I give 'em all sweet spit of nitre
For that, myself: that sometimes cures."
"Now, Beauty, mind them feet of yours."
They groomed, and sissed with hissing notes
To keep the dust out of their throats.

There came again and yet again
The feed-box lid, the swish of grain,
Or Joe's boots stamping in the loft,
The hay-fork's stab and then the soft
Hay's scratching slither down the shoot.
Then with a thud some horse's foot
Stamped, and the gulping munch again
Resumed its lippings at the grain.

The road outside the inn was quiet
Save for the poor, mad, restless pyat
Hopping his hanging wicker-cage.
No calmative of sleep or sage
Will cure the fever to be free.
He shook the wicker ceaselessly
Now up, now down, but never out
On wind-waves, being blown about,
Looking for dead things good to eat.
His cage was strewn with scattered wheat.

At ten o'clock, the Doctor's lad
Brought up his master's hunting pad

And put him in a stall, and leaned
Against the stall, and sissed, and cleaned
The port and cannons of his curb.
He chewed a sprig of smelling herb.
He sometimes stopped, and spat, and chid
The silly things his master did.

At twenty past, old Baldock strode
His ploughman's straddle down the road.
An old man with a gaunt, burnt face;
His eyes rapt back on some far place,
Like some starved, half-mad saint in bliss
In God's world through the rags of this.
He leaned upon a stake of ash
Cut from a sapling: many a gash
Was in his old, full-skirted coat.
The twisted muscles in his throat
Moved, as he swallowed, like taut cord.
His oaken face was seamed and gored.
He halted by the inn and stared
On that far bliss, that place prepared
Beyond his eyes, beyond his mind.

Then Thomas Copp, of Cowfoot's Wynd,
Drove up; and stopped to take a glass.
"I hope they'll gallop on my grass,"
He said, "My little girl does sing
To see the red goats galloping.
It's good for grass, too, to be trodden
Except they poach it, where it's sodden."
Then Billy Waldrist, from the Lynn,
With Jockey Hill, from Pitts, came in
And had a sip of gin and stout
To help the jockey's sweatings out.
"Rare day for scent," the jockey said.

A pony like a feather bed
On four short sticks, took place aside.
The little girl who rode astride
Watched everything with eyes that glowed
With glory in the horse she rode.

At half-past ten, some lads on foot
Came to be beaters to a shoot
Of rabbits at the Warren Hill.
Rough sticks they had, and Hob and Jill,
Their ferrets, in a bag, and netting.
They talked of dinner-beer and betting;
And jeered at those who stood around.
They rolled their dogs upon the ground
And teased them: "Rats"; they cried, "go fetch."
"Go seek, good Roxer; 'z bite, good betch.
What dinner-beer'll they give us, lad?
Sex quarts the lot last year we had.
They'd ought to give us seven this.
Seek, Susan; what a betch it is."

A pommle cob came trotting up
Round-bellied like a drinking-cup
Bearing on back a pommle man
Round-bellied like a drinking-can.
The clergyman from Condicote.
His face was scarlet from his trot,
His white hair bobbed about his head
As halos do round clergy dead.
He asked Tom Copp, "How long to wait?"
His loose mouth opened like a gate,
To pass the wagons of his speech,
He had a mighty voice to preach
Though indolent in other matters
He let his children go in tatters.

His daughter Madge on foot, flush-cheekt,
In broken hat and boots that leakt,
With bits of hay all over her,
Her plain face grinning at the stir
(A broad pale face, snub-nosed, with speckles
Of sandy eyebrows sprinkt with freckles)
Came after him and stood apart
Beside the darling of her heart,
Miss Hattie Dyce from Baydon Dean;
A big young fair one, chiselled clean,
Brow, chin and nose, with great blue eyes,
All innocence and sweet surprise,
And golden hair piled coil on coil
Too beautiful for time to spoil.
They talked in undertones together
Not of the hunting, nor the weather.
Old Steven from Scratch Steven Place,
(A white beard and a rosy face),
Came next on his stringhalty grey,
"I've come to see the hounds away,"
He said, "And ride a field or two.
We old have better things to do
Than breaking all our necks for fun."
He shone on people like the sun,
And on himself for shining so.

Three men came riding in a row:—
John Pym, a bull-man, quick to strike,
Gross and blunt-headed like a shrike
Yet sweet-voiced as a piping flute;
Tom See, the trainer, from the Toot,
Red, with an angry, puzzled face
And mouth twitched upward out of place,
Sucking cheap grapes and spitting seeds;
And Stone, of Bartle's Cattle Feeds,

A man whose bulk of flesh and bone
Made people call him Twenty Stone.
He was the man who stood a pull
At Tencombe with the Jersey bull
And brought the bull back to his stall.

Some children ranged the tavern-wall.
Sucking their thumbs and staring hard;
Some grooms brought horses from the yard.
Jane Selbie said to Ellen Tranter,
"A lot on 'em come doggin', ant her?"
"A lot on 'em," said Ellen, "look
There'm Mr. Gaunt of Water's Hook.
They say he" . . . (whispered). "Law," said Jane.
Gaunt flung his heel across the mane,
And slithered from his horse and stamped.
"Boots tight," he said, "my feet are cramped."

A loose-shod horse came clicking clack;
Nick Wolvesey on a hired hack
Come tittup, like a cup and ball.
One saw the sun, moon, stars and all
The great green earth twixt him and saddle;
Then Molly Wolvesey riding straddle
Red as a rose, with eyes like sparks,
Two boys from college out for larks
Hunted bright Molly for a smile
But were not worth their quarry's while.

Two eyeglassed gunners dressed in tweed
Came with a spaniel on a lead
And waited for a fellow gunner.
The parson's son, the famous runner,
Came dressed to follow hounds on foot.
His knees were red as yew tree root

From being bare, day in day out;
He wore a blazer, and a clout
(His sweater's arms) tied round his neck.
His football shorts had many a speck
And splash of mud from many a fall
Got as he picked the slippery ball
Heeled out behind a breaking scrum.
He grinned at people, but was dumb,
Not like these lousy foreigners.
The otter-hounds and harriers
From Godstow to the Wye all knew him.

And with him came the stock which grew him
The parson and his sporting wife,
She was a stout one, full of life
With red, quick, kindly, manly face.
She held the knave, queen, king and ace,
In every hand she played with men.
She was no sister to the hen,
But fierce and minded to be queen.
She wore a coat and skirt of green,
A waistcoat cut of hunting red,
Her tie pin was a fox's head.

The parson was a manly one
His jolly eyes were bright with fun.
His jolly mouth was well inclined
To cry aloud his jolly mind
To everyone, in jolly terms.
He did not talk of churchyard worms,
But of our privilege as dust
To box a lively bout with lust
Ere going to Heaven to rejoice.
He loved the sound of his own voice.
His talk was like a charge of horse;

His build was all compact, for force,
Well-knit, well-made, well-coloured, eager,
He kept no Lent to make him meagre.
He loved his God, himself and man.
He never said "life's wretched span;
This wicked world," in any sermon.
This body that we feed the worm on,
To him, was jovial stuff that thrilled.
He liked to see the foxes killed;
But most he felt himself in clover
To hear "Hen left, hare right, cock over,"
At woodside, when the leaves are brown.
Some grey cathedral in a town
Where drowsy bells toll out the time
To shaven closes sweet with lime,
And wall-flower roots drive out of the mortar
All summer on the Norman Dortar,
Was certain some day to be his.
Nor would a mitre go amiss
To him, because he governed well.
His voice was like the tenor bell
When services were said and sung.
And he had read in many a tongue,
Arabic, Hebrew, Spanish, Greek.

Two bright young women, nothing meek,
Rode up on bicycles and propped
Their wheels in such wise that they dropped
To bring the parson's son to aid.
Their cycling suits were tailor-made,
Smart, mannish, pert, but feminine.
The colour and the zest of wine
Were in their presence and their bearing;
Like spring, they brought the thought of pairing.
The parson's lady thought them pert.

And they could mock a man and flirt,
Do billiard tricks with corks and pennies,
Sing ragtime songs and win at tennis
The silver-cigarette-case-prize.
They had good colour and bright eyes,
Bright hair, bright teeth and pretty skin,
Which many lads had longed to win
On darkened stairways after dances.
Their reading was the last romances,
And they were dashing hockey players
Men called them, "Jill and Joan, the slayers."
They were as bright as fresh sweet-peas.
Old Farmer Bennett followed these
Upon his big-boned savage black
Whose mule-teeth yellowed to bite back
Whatever came within his reach.
Old Bennett sat him like a leech
The grim old rider seemed to be
As hard about the mouth as he.

The beaters nudged each other's ribs
With "There he goes, his bloody Nibs.
He come on Joe and Anty Cop,
And beat 'em with his hunting crop
Like tho' they'd bin a sack of beans.
His pickers were a pack of queans,
And Joe and Anty took a couple
He caught 'em there, and banged 'em supple.
Women and men, he didn't care
(He'd kill 'em some day, if he dare)
He beat the whole four nearly dead.
'I'll learn 'ee rabbit in my shed,
That's how my ricks get set afire.'
That's what he said, the bloody liar;
Old oaf, I'd like to burn his ricks,

Th' old swine's too free with fists and sticks.
He keeps that Mrs. Jones himselve."

Just like an axehead on its helve
Old Bennett sat and watched the gathering.
He'd given many a man a lathering
In field or barn, and women, too.
His cold eye reached the women through
With comment, and the men with scorn.
He hated women gently born;
He hated all beyond his grasp;
For he was minded like the asp
That strikes whatever is not dust.

Charles Copse, of Copse Hold Manor, thrust
Next into view.   In face and limb
The beauty and the grace of him
Were like the golden age returned.
His grave eyes steadily discerned
The good in men and what was wise.
He had deep blue, mild-coloured eyes,
And shocks of harvest-coloured hair,
Still beautiful with youth.   An air
Or power of kindness went about him;
No heart of youth could ever doubt him
Or fail to follow where he led.
He was a genius, simply bred,
And quite unconscious of his power.
He was the very red rose flower
Of all that coloured countryside.
Gauchos had taught him how to ride.
He knew all arts, but practised most
The art of bettering flesh and ghost
In men and lads down in the mud.
He knew no class in flesh and blood.

He loved his kind. He spent some pith
Long since, relieving Ladysmith.
Many a horse he trotted tame,
Heading commandos from their aim,
In those old days upon the veldt.
An old bear in a scarlet pelt
Came next, old Squire Harridew,
His eyebrows gave a man the grue
So bushy and so fierce they were;
He had a bitter tongue to swear.
A fierce, hot, hard, old, stupid squire,
With all his liver made of fire,
Small brain, great courage, mulish will.
The hearts in all his house stood still
When someone crossed the squire's path.
For he was terrible in wrath,
And smashed whatever came to hand.
Two things he failed to understand,
The foreigner and what was new.

His daughters, Carrie, Jane and Lu
Rode with him, Carrie at his side.
His son, the ne'er-do-weel, had died
In Arizona, long before.
The Squire set the greatest store
By Carrie, youngest of the three,
And lovely to the blood was she;
Blonde, with a face of blush and cream,
And eyes deep violet in their gleam,
Bright blue when quiet in repose.
She was a very golden rose.
And many a man when sunset came
Would see the manor windows flame,
And think, "My beauty's home is there."
Queen Helen had less golden hair,

Queen Cleopatra paler lips,
Queen Blanche's eyes were in eclipse,
By golden Carrie's glancing by.
She had a wit for mockery
And sang mild, pretty senseless songs
Of sunsets, Heav'n and lover's wrongs,
Sweet to the Squire when he had dined.
A rosebud need not have a mind.
A lily is not sweet from learning.
Jane looked like a dark lantern, burning.
Outwardly dark, unkempt, uncouth,
But minded like the living truth,
A friend that nothing shook nor wearied.
She was not "Darling Jane'd," nor "dearie'd,"
She was all prickles to the touch,
So sharp, that many feared to clutch,
So keen, that many thought her bitter.
She let the little sparrows twitter.
She had a hard ungracious way.
Her storm of hair was iron-grey,
And she was passionate in her heart
For women's souls that burn apart,
Just as her mother's had, with Squire.
She gave the sense of smouldering fire.
She was not happy being a maid,
At home, with Squire, but she stayed
Enduring life, however bleak,
To guard her sisters who were weak,
And force a life for them from Squire.
And she had roused and stood his fire
A hundred times, and earned his hate,
To win those two a better state.
Long years before the Canon's son
Had cared for her, but he had gone
To Klondyke, to the mines, for gold,

To find, in some strange way untold
A foreign grave that no men knew.

No depth, nor beauty, was in Lu,
But charm and fun, for she was merry,
Round, sweet and little like a cherry,
With laughter like a robin's singing;
She was not kittenlike and clinging,
But pert and arch and fond of flirting,
In mocking ways that were not hurting,
And merry ways that women pardoned.
Not being married yet she gardened.
She loved sweet music; she would sing
Songs made before the German King
Made England German in her mind.
She sang "My lady is unkind,"
"The Hunt is up," and those sweet things
Which Thomas Campion set to strings
"Thrice toss," and "What," and "Where are now?"

The next to come was Major Howe
Driv'n in a dog-cart by a groom.
The testy major was in fume
To find no hunter standing waiting;
The groom who drove him caught a rating,
The groom who had the horse in stable,
Was damned in half the tongues of Babel.
The Major being hot and heady
When horse or dinner was not ready.
He was a lean, tough, liverish fellow,
With pale blue eyes (the whites pale yellow),
Moustache clipped toothbrush-wise, and jaws
Shaved bluish like old partridge claws.
When he had stripped his coat he made
A speckless presence for parade,

New pink, white cords, and glossy tops
New gloves, the newest thing in crops,
Worn with an air that well expressed
His sense that no one else was dressed.

Quick trotting after Major Howe
Came Doctor Frome of Quickemshow,
A smiling silent man whose brain
Knew all of every secret pain
In every man and woman there.
Their inmost lives were all laid bare
To him, because he touched their lives
When strong emotions sharp as knives
Brought out what sort of soul each was.
As secret as the graveyard grass
He was, as he had need to be.
At some time he had had to see
Each person there, sans clothes, sans mask,
Sans lying even, when to ask
Probed a tamed spirit into truth.

Richard, his son, a jolly youth
Rode with him, fresh from Thomas's,
As merry as a yearling is
In maytime in a clover patch.
He was a gallant chick to hatch
Big, brown and smiling, blithe and kind,
With all his father's love of mind
And greater force to give it act.
To see him when the scrum was packt,
Heave, playing forward, was a sight.
His tackling was the crowd's delight
In many a danger close to goal.
The pride in the three quarter's soul
Dropped, like a wet rag, when he collared.
He was as steady as a bollard,

And gallant as a skysail yard.
He rode a chestnut mare which sparred.
In good St. Thomas' Hospital,
He was the crown imperial
Of all the scholars of his year.

The Harold lads, from Tencombe Weir,
Came all on foot in corduroys,
Poor widowed Mrs. Harold's boys,
Dick, Hal and Charles, whose father died.
(Will Masemore shot him in the side
By accident at Masemore Farm
A hazel knocked Will Masemore's arm
In getting through a hedge; his gun
Was not half-cocked, so it was done
And those three boys left fatherless.)
Their gaitered legs were in a mess
With good red mud from twenty ditches
Hal's face was plastered like his breeches
Dick chewed a twig of juniper.
They kept at distance from the stir
Their loss had made them lads apart.
Next came the Colway's pony cart
From Coln St. Evelyn's with the party
Hugh Colway jovial, bold and hearty
And Polly Colway's brother, John
(Their horses had been both sent on)
And Polly Colway drove them there.
Poor pretty Polly Colway's hair.
The grey mare killed her at the brook
Down Seven Springs Mead at Water Hook,
Just one month later, poor sweet woman.
Her brother was a rat-faced Roman
Lean, puckered, tight-skinned from the sea
Commander in the *Canace*

Able to drive a horse, or ship,
Or crew of men, without a whip
By will, as long as they could go.
His face would wrinkle, row on row,
From mouth to hair-roots when he laught
He looked ahead as though his craft
Were with him still, in dangerous channels.
He and Hugh Colway tossed their flannels
Into the pony-cart and mounted.
Six foiled attempts the watchers counted,
The horses being bickering things,
That so much scarlet made like kings,
Such sidling and such pawing and shifting.

When Hugh was up his mare went drifting
Sidelong and feeling with her heels
For horses' legs and poshay wheels,
While lather creamed her neat clipt skin.
Hugh guessed her foibles with a grin.
He was a rich town-merchant's son,
A wise and kind man fond of fun,
Who loved to have a troop of friends
At Coln St. Eves for all week-ends,
And troops of children in for tea
He gloried in a Christmas Tree.
And Polly was his heart's best treasure,
And Polly was a golden pleasure
To everyone, to see or hear.

Poor Polly's dying struck him queer,
He was a darkened man thereafter,
Cowed silent, he would wince at laughter
And be so gentle it was strange
Even to see.   Life loves to change.

Now Coln St. Evelyn's hearths are cold
The shutters up, the hunters sold,

And green mould damps the locked front door.
But this was still a month before,
And Polly, golden in the chaise,
Still smiled, and there were golden days,
Still thirty days, for those dear lovers.

The Riddens came, from Ocle Covers,
Bill Ridden riding Stormalong,
(By Tempest out of Love-me-long)
A proper handful of a horse,
That nothing but the Aintree course
Could bring to terms, save Bill perhaps.
All sport, from bloody war to craps,
Came well to Bill, that big-mouthed smiler;
They nick-named him "the mug-beguiler",
For Billy lived too much with horses
In coper's yards and sharper's courses,
To lack the sharper-coper streak.
He did not turn the other cheek,
When struck (as English Christians do),
He boxed like a Whitechapel Jew,
And many a time his knuckles bled
Against a race-course-gipsy's head.
For "hit him first and argue later,"
Was truth at Billy's alma mater,
Not love, not any bosh of love.
His hand was like a chamois glove
And riding was his chief delight.
He bred the chaser Chinese-white,
From Lilybud by Mandarin.
And when his mouth tucked corners in,
And scent was high and hounds were going.
He went across a field like snowing
And tackled anything that came.

His wife, Sal Ridden, was the same,
A loud, bold, blonde abundant mare,
With white horse teeth and stooks of hair,
(Like polished brass) and such a manner
It flaunted from her like a banner.
Her father was Tom See the trainer;
She rode a lovely earth-disdainer
Which she and Billy wished to sell.

Behind them rode her daughter Bell,
A strange shy lovely girl whose face
Was sweet with thought and proud with race,
And bright with joy at riding there.
She was as good as blowing air
But shy and difficult to know
The kittens in the barley-mow,
The setter's toothless puppies sprawling,
The blackbird in the apple calling,
All knew her spirit more than we
So delicate these maidens be
In loving lovely helpless things.

The Manor set, from Tencombe Rings,
Came, with two friends, a set of six.
Ed Manor with his cockerel chicks,
Nob, Cob and Bunny as they called them,
(God help the school or rule which galled them;
They carried head) and friends from town.

Ed Manor trained on Tencombe Down.
He once had been a famous bat,
He had that stroke, "the Manor-pat,"
Which snicked the ball for three, past cover.
He once scored twenty in an over,
But now he cricketed no more.
He purpled in the face and swore

At all three sons, and trained, and told
Long tales of cricketing of old,
When he alone had saved his side.
Drink made it doubtful if he lied,
Drink purpled him, he could not face
The fences now, nor go the pace
He brought his friends to meet; no more.

His big son Nob, at whom he swore,
Swore back at him, for Nob was surly,
Tall, shifty, sullen-smiling, burly,
Quite fearless, built with such a jaw
That no man's rule could be his law
Nor any woman's son his master.
Boxing he relished. He could plaster
All those who boxed out Tencombe way
A front tooth had been knocked away
Two days before, which put his mouth
A little to the east of south.
And put a venom in his laughter.

Cob was a lighter lad, but dafter;
Just past eighteen, while Nob was twenty.
Nob had no nerves but Cob had plenty
So Cobby went where Nobby led.
He had no brains inside his head,
Was fearless, just like Nob, but put
Some clog of folly round his foot,
Where Nob put will of force or fraud;
He spat aside and muttered Gawd
When vext; he took to whiskey kindly
And loved and followed Nobby blindly,
And rode as in the saddle born.

Bun looked upon the two with scorn
He was the youngest, and was wise.

He, too, was fair, with sullen eyes,
He too (a year before) had had
A zest for going to the bad,
With Cob and Nob. He knew the joys
Of drinking with the stable-boys,
Or smoking while he filled his skin
With pints of Guinness dashed with gin
And Cobby yelled a bawdy ditty,
Or cutting Nobby for the kitty,
And damning peoples' eyes and guts,
Or drawing evening-church for sluts
He knew them all and now was quit.

Sweet Polly Colway managed it.
And Bunny changed. He dropped his drink,
(The pleasant pit's seductive brink),
He started working in the stable,
And well, for he was shrewd and able.
He left the doubtful female friends
Picked up at Evening-Service ends,
He gave up cards and swore no more.
Nob called him "the Reforming Whore,"
"The Soul's Awakening," or "The Text,"
Nob being always coarse when vext.

Ed Manor's friends were Hawke and Sladd,
Old college friends, the last he had,
Rare horsemen, but their nerves were shaken
By all the whiskey they had taken.
Hawke's hand was trembling on his rein.
His eyes were dead-blue like a vein,
His peaked sad face was touched with breeding,
His querulous mind was quaint from reading,
His piping voice still quirked with fun.
Many a mad thing he had done,
Riding to hounds and going to races.

A glimmer of the gambler's graces,
Wit, courage, devil, touched his talk.

Sladd's big fat face was white as chalk,
His mind went wandering, swift yet solemn,
Twixt winning-post and betting column,
The weights and forms and likely colts.
He said "This road is full of jolts.
I shall be seasick riding here.
O damn last night with that liqueur."

Len Stokes rode up on Peterkin;
He owned the Downs by Baydon Whin;
And grazed some thousand sheep; the boy
Grinned round at men with jolly joy
At being alive and being there.
His big round face and mop of hair
Shone, his great teeth shone in his grin,
The clean blood in his clear tanned skin
Ran merry, and his great voice mocked
His young friends present till they rocked.

Steer Harpit came from Rowell Hill,
A small, frail man, all heart and will,
A sailor as his voice betrayed.
He let his whip-thong droop and played
At snicking off the grass-blades with it.
John Hankerton, from Compton Lythitt,
Was there with Pity Hankerton,
And Mike, their good-for-little-son,
Back, smiling, from his seventh job.
Joan Urch was there upon her cob.
Tom Sparsholt on his lanky grey.
John Restrop from Hope Goneaway.
And Vaughan, the big black handsome devil,
Loose-lipped with song and wine and revel
All rosy from his morning tub.

The Godsdown tigress with her cub
(Lady and Tommy Crowmarsh) came.
The great eyes smouldered in the dame,
Wit glittered, too, which few men saw.
There was more beauty there than claw.
Tommy in bearing, horse and dress
Was black, fastidious, handsomeness,
Choice to his trimmed soul's fingertips.
Heredia's sonnets on his lips.
A line undrawn, a plate not bitten,
A stone uncut, a phrase unwritten,
That would be perfect, made his mind.
A choice pull, from a rare print, signed,
Was Tommy. He collected plate,
(Old Sheffield) and he owned each state
Of all the Meryon Paris etchings.
Colonel Sir Button Budd of Fletchings
Was there; Long Robert Thrupp was there,
(Three yards of him men said there were),
Long as the King of Prussia's fancy.
He rode the longlegged Necromancy,
A useless racehorse that could canter.
George Childrey with his jolly banter
Was there, Nick Childrey, too, come down
The night before from London town,
To hunt and have his lungs blown clean.
The Ilsley set from Tuttocks Green
Was there (old Henry Ilsley drove),
Carlotta Ilsely brought her love
A flop-jowled broker from the city.
Men pitied her, for she was pretty.

Some grooms and second horsemen mustered.
A lot of men on foot were clustered
Round the inn-door, all busy drinking,

One heard the kissing glasses clinking
In passage as the tray was brought.
Two terriers (which they had there) fought
There on the green, a loud, wild whirl.
Bell stopped them like a gallant girl.
The hens behind the tavern clucked.

Then on a horse which bit and bucked
(The half-broke four-year-old Marauder)
Came Minton-Price of th' Afghan border
Lean, puckered, yellowed, knotted, scarred,
Tough as a hide-rope twisted hard,
Tense tiger-sinew knit to bone.
Strange-wayed from having lived alone
With Kafir, Afghan and Beloosh
In stations frozen in the Koosh
Where nothing but the bullet sings.
His mind had conquered many things
Painting, mechanics, physics, law,
White-hot, hand-beaten things to draw
Self-hammered from his own soul's stithy,
His speech was blacksmith-sparked and pithy.
Danger had been his brother bred;
The stones had often been his bed
In bickers with the border-thieves.

A chestnut mare with swerves and heaves
Came plunging, scattering all the crowd,
She tossed her head and laughed aloud
And bickered sideways past the meet.
From pricking ears to mincing feet
She was all tense with blood and quiver
You saw her clipt hide twitch and shiver
Over her netted cords of veins.
She carried Cothill, of the Sleins;

A tall, black, bright-eyed handsome lad.
Great power and great grace he had.
Men hoped the greatest things of him,
His grace made people think him slim,
But he was muscled like a horse
A sculptor would have wrought his torse
In bronze or marble for Apollo.
He loved to hurry like a swallow
For miles on miles of short-grassed sweet
Blue-harebelled downs where dewy feet
Of pure winds hurry ceaselessly.
He loved the downland like a sea,
The downland where the kestrels hover;
The downland had him for a lover.
And every other thing he loved
In which a clean free spirit moved.

So beautiful, he was, so bright.
He looked to men like young delight
Gone courting April maidenhood,
That has the primrose in her blood,
He on his mincing lady mare.

Ock Gurney and old Pete were there,
Riding their bonny cobs and swearing.
Ock's wife had giv'n them both a fairing,
A horse-rosette, red, white and blue.
Their cheeks were brown as any brew,
And every comer to the meet
Said "Hello, Ock" or "Morning, Pete;
Be you a going to a wedding?"
"Why, noa," they said, "we'm going a bedding;
Now ben't us, uncle, ben't us, Ock?"
Pete Gurney was a lusty cock
Turned sixty-three, but bright and hale,
A dairy-farmer in the vale,

Much like a robin in the face,
Much character in little space,
With little eyes like burning coal.
His mouth was like a slit or hole
In leather that was seamed and lined.
He had the russet-apple mind
That betters as the weather worsen.
He was a manly English person,
Kind to the core, brave, merry, true;
One grief he had, a grief still new,
That former Parson joined with Squire
In putting down the Playing Quire,
In church, and putting organ in.
"Ah, boys, that was a pious din
That Quire was; a pious praise
The noise was that we used to raise;
I and my serpent, George with his'n,
On Easter Day in He is Risen,
Or blessed Christmas in Venite;
And how the trombone came in mighty,
In Alleluias from the heart.
Pious, for each man played his part,
Not like 'tis now." Thus he, still sore
For changes forty years before,
When all (that could) in time and tune,
Blew trumpets to the newë moon.
He was a bachelor, from choice.
He and his nephew farmed the Boyce
Prime pasture land for thirty cows.
Ock's wife, Selina Jane, kept house,
And jolly were the three together.

Ock had a face like summer weather
A broad red sun, split by a smile.
He mopped his forehead all the while,

And said "By damn," and Ben't us, Unk?"
His eyes were close and deeply sunk.
He cursed his hunter like a lover,
"Now blast your soul, my dear, give over.
Woa, now, my pretty, damn your eyes."
Like Pete he was of middle size,
Dean-oak-like, stuggy, strong in shoulder,
He stood a wrestle like a boulder,
He had a back for pitching hay.
His singing voice was like a bay.
In talk he had a sideways spit,
Each minute, to refresh his wit.
He cracked Brazil nuts with this teeth.
He challenged Cobbett of the Heath
(Weight-lifting champion) once, but lost.
Hunting was what he loved the most,
Next to his wife and Uncle Pete.
With beer to drink and cheese to eat,
And rain in May to fill the grasses,
This life was not a dream that passes
To Ock, but like the summer flower.
But now the clock had struck the hour,
And round the corner, down the road
The bob-bob-bobbing serpent flowed
With three black knobs upon its spine;
Three bobbing black-caps in a line.
A glimpse of scarlet at the gap
Showed underneath each bobbing cap,
And at the corner by the gate,
One heard Tom Dansey give a rate,
"Hep, Drop it, Jumper; have a care"
There came a growl, half-rate, half-swear,
A spitting crack, a tuneful whimper
And sweet religion entered Jumper.

There was a general turn of faces,
The men and horses shifted places,
And round the corner came the hunt,
Those feathery things, the hounds, in front,
Intent, wise, dipping, trotting, straying,
Smiling at people, shoving, playing,
Nosing to children's faces, waving
Their feathery sterns, and all behaving,
One eye to Dansey on Maroon.
Their padding cat-feet beat a tune,
And though they trotted up so quiet
Their noses brought them news of riot,
Wild smells of things with living blood,
Hot smells, against the grippers good,
Of weasel, rabbit, cat and hare,
Whose feet had been before them there,
Whose taint still tingled every breath;
But Dansey on Maroon was death,
So, though their noses roved, their feet
Larked and trit-trotted to the meet.

Bill Tall and Ell and Mirtie Key
(Aged fourteen years between the three)
Were flooded by them at the bend,
They thought their little lives would end,
For grave sweet eyes looked into theirs,
Cold noses came, and clean short hairs
And tails all crumpled up like ferns,
A sea of moving heads and sterns,
All round them, brushing coat and dress:
One paused, expecting a caress.
The children shrank into each other,
Shut eyes, clutched tight, and shouted "Mother"
With mouths wide open, catching tears.

Sharp Mrs. Tall allayed their fears,
"Err out the road, the dogs won't hurt 'ee.
There now, you've cried your faces dirty.
More cleaning up for me to do.
What? Cry at dogs, great lumps like you?"
She licked her handkerchief and smeared
Their faces where the dirt appeared.

The hunt trit-trotted to the meeting,
Tom Dansey touching cap to greeting,
Slow-lifting crop-thong to the rim,
No hunter there got more from him
Except some brightening of the eye.
He halted at the Cock and Pye,
The hounds drew round him on the green,
Arrogant, Daffodil and Queen,
Closest, but all in little space.
Some lolled their tongues, some made grimace,
Yawning, or tilting nose in quest,
All stood and looked about with zest,
They were uneasy as they waited.
Their sires and dams had been well-mated,
They were a lovely pack for looks;
Their forelegs drumsticked without crooks,
Straight, without overtread or bend,
Muscled to gallop to the end,
With neat feet round as any cat's.
Great chested, muscled in the slats,
Bright, clean, short-coated, broad in shoulder
With stag-like eyes that seemed to smoulder.
The heads well-cocked, the clean necks strong;
Brows broad, ears close, the muzzles long;
And all like racers in the thighs;
Their noses exquisitely wise,
Their minds being memories of smells;

Their voices like a ring of bells;
Their sterns all spirit, cock and feather;
Their colours like the English weather,
Magpie and hare, and badger-pye,
Like minglings in a double dye,
Some smutty-nosed, some tan, none bald;
Their manners were to come when called,
Their flesh was sinew knit to bone,
Their courage like a banner blown.
Their joy, to push him out of cover,
And hunt him till they rolled him over.
They were as game as Robert Dover.
Tom Dansey was a famous whip
Trained as a child in horsemanship
Entered, as soon as he was able
As boy at Caunter's racing stable;
There, like the other boys, he slept
In stall beside the horse he kept,
Snug in the straw; and Caunter's stick
Brought morning to him all too quick.
He learned the high quick gingery ways
Of thoroughbreds; his stable days
Made him a rider, groom and vet.
He promised to be too thickset
For jockeying, so left it soon.
Now he was whip and rode Maroon.

He was a small, lean, wiry man
With sunk cheeks weathered to a tan
Scarred by the spikes of hawthorn sprays
Dashed thro', head down, on going days,
In haste to see the line they took.
There was a beauty in his look
It was intent.   His speech was plain.
Maroon's head, reaching to the rein,

Had half his thought before he spoke.
His "gone away," when foxes broke,
Was like a bell. His chief delight
Was hunting fox from noon to night.
His pleasure lay in hounds and horses,
He loved the Seven Springs water-courses,
Those flashing brooks (in good sound grass,
Where scent would hang like breath on glass).
He loved the English countryside;
The wine-leaved bramble in the ride,
The lichen on the apple-trees,
The poultry ranging on the lees,
The farms, the moist earth-smelling cover,
His wife's green grave at Mitcheldover,
Where snowdrops pushed at the first thaw.
Under his hide his heart was raw
With joy and pity of these things.
The second whip was Kitty Myngs
Still but a lad but keen and quick
(Son of old Myngs who farmed the Wick)
A horse-mouthed lad who knew his work.
He rode the big black horse, the Turk,
And longed to be a huntsman bold.
He had the horse-look, sharp and old,
With much good-nature in his face.
His passion was to go the pace
His blood was crying for a taming.
He was the Devil's chick for gaming,
He was a rare good lad to box.
He sometimes had a main of cocks
Down at the Flags. His job with hounds
At present kept his blood in bounds
From rioting and running hare.
Tom Dansey made him have a care
He worshipped Dansey heart and soul.

To be a huntsman was his goal
To be with hounds, to charge full tilt
Blackthorns that made the gentry wilt
Was his ambition and his hope.
He was a hot colt needing rope
He was too quick to speak his passion
To suit his present huntsman's fashion.

The huntsman, Robin Dawe, looked round,
He sometimes called a favourite hound,
Gently, to see the creature turn
Look happy up and wag his stern.
He smiled and nodded and saluted,
To those who hailed him, as it suited.
And patted Pip's, his hunter's neck.
His new pink was without a speck;
He was a red-faced smiling fellow,
His voice clear tenor, full and mellow,
His eyes, all fire, were black and small.
He had been smashed in many a fall.
His eyebrow had a white curved mark
Left by the bright shoe of The Lark,
Down in a ditch by Seven Springs.
His coat had all been trod to strings,
His ribs laid bare and shoulder broken
Being jumped on down at Water's Oaken,
The time his horse came down and rolled.
His face was of the country mould
Such as the mason sometimes cutted
On English moulding-ends which jutted
Out of the church walls, centuries since.
And as you never know the quince,
How good he is, until you try,
So, in Dawe's face, what met the eye
Was only part, what lay behind

Was English character and mind.
Great kindness, delicate sweet feeling,
(Most shy, most clever in concealing
Its depth) for beauty of all sorts,
Great manliness and love of sports,
A grave wise thoughtfulness and truth,
A merry fun, outlasting youth,
A courage terrible to see
And mercy for his enemy.

He had a clean-shaved face, but kept
A hedge of whisker neatly clipt,
A narrow strip or picture frame
(Old Dawe, the woodman, did the same),
Under his chin from ear to ear.

But now the resting hounds gave cheer,
Joyful and Arrogant and Catch-him,
Smelt the glad news and ran to snatch him,
The Master's dogcart turned the bend.
Damsel and Skylark knew their friend;
A thrill ran through the pack like fire,
And little whimpers ran in quire.
The horses cocked and pawed and whickered,
Young Cothill's chaser kicked and bickered,
And stood on end and struck out sparks.
Joyful and Catch-him sang like larks,
There was the Master in the trap,
Clutching old Roman in his lap,
Old Roman, crazy for his brothers,
And putting frenzy in the others,
To set them at the dogcart wheels,
With thrusting heads and little squeals.

The Master put old Roman by,
And eyed the thrusters heedfully,

He called a few pet hounds and fed
Three special friends with scraps of bread,
Then peeled his wraps, climbed down and strod
Through all those clamourers in the road,
Saluted friends, looked round the crowd,
Saw Harridew's three girls and bowed,
Then took White Rabbit from the groom.

He was Sir Peter Bynd, of Coombe;
Past sixty now, though hearty still,
A living picture of good-will,
An old, grave soldier, sweet and kind,
A courtier with a knightly mind,
Who felt whatever thing he thought.
His face was scarred, for he had fought
Five wars for us.　Within his face
Courage and power had their place,
Rough energy, decision, force.
He smiled about him from his horse.
He had a welcome and salute
For all, on horse or wheel or foot,
Whatever kind of life each followed.
His tanned, drawn cheeks looked old and hollowed,
But still his bright blue eyes were young,
And when the pack crashed into tongue,
And staunch White Rabbit shook like fire,
He sent him at it like a flier,
And lived with hounds while horses could.
"They'm lying in the Ghost Heath Wood,
Sir Peter," said an earth-stopper,
(Old Baldy Hill), "You'll find 'em there.
'Z I come'd across I smell 'em plain.
There's one up back, down Tuttock's drain,
But, Lord, it's just a bog, the Tuttocks,
Hounds would be swallered to the buttocks.

Heath Wood, Sir Peter's best to draw."
Sir Peter gave two minutes' law
For Kingston Challow and his daughter;
He said. "They're late. We'll start the slaughter.
Ghost Heath, then, Dansey. We'll be going."

Now, at his word, the tide was flowing
Off went Maroon, off went the hounds,
Down road, then off, to Chols Elm Grounds,
Across soft turf with dead leaves cleaving
And hillocks that the mole was heaving,
Mild going to those trotting feet.
After the scarlet coats, the meet
Came clopping up the grass in spate
They poached the trickle at the gate;
Their horses' feet sucked at the mud;
Excitement in the horses' blood,
Cocked forward every ear and eye;
They quivered as the hounds went by,
They trembled when they first trod grass;
They would not let another pass
They scattered wide up Chols Elm Hill.

The wind was westerly but still;
The sky a high fair-weather cloud,
Like meadows ridge-and-furrow ploughed,
Just glinting sun but scarcely moving.
Blackbirds and thrushes thought of loving,
Catkins were out; the day seemed tense
It was so still. At every fence
Cow-parsley pushed its thin green fern.
White-violet-leaves shewed at the burn.

Young Cothill let his chaser go
Round Chols Elm Field a turn or so
To soothe his edge. The riders went

Chatting and laughing and content
In groups of two or three together.
The hounds, a flock of shaking feather,
Bobbed on ahead, past Chols Elm Cop.
The horses' shoes went clip-a-clop,
Along the stony cart-track there.
The little spinney was all bare,
But in the earth-moist winter day
The scarlet coats twixt tree and spray,
The glistening horses pressing on,
The brown faced lads, Bill, Dick and John,
And all the hurry to arrive,
Were beautiful like spring alive.
The hounds melted away with Master
The tanned lads ran, the field rode faster,
The chatter joggled in the throats
Of riders bumping by like boats,
"We really ought to hunt a bye day."
"Fine day for scent," "A fly or die day."
"They chopped a bagman in the check,
He had a collar round his neck."
"Old Ridden's girl's a pretty flapper."
"That Vaughan's a cad, the whipper-snapper."
"I tell 'ee, lads, I seed 'em plain,
Down in the Rough at Shifford's Main,
Old Squire stamping like a duke,
So red with blood I thought he'd puke,
In appleplexie, as they do.

Miss Jane stood just as white as dew,
And heard him out in just white heat,
And then she trimmed him down a treat,
About Miss Lou it was, or Carrie
(She'd be a pretty peach to marry)."

"Her'll draw up-wind, so us'll go
Down by the furze, we'll see 'em so."

"Look, there they go, lad."

            There they went,
Across the brook and up the bent,
Past Primrose Wood, past Brady Ride,
Along Ghost Heath to cover side.
The bobbing scarlet, trotting pack,
Turf scatters tossed behind each back,
Some horses blowing with a whinny,
A jam of horses in the spinney,
Close to the ride-gate; leather straining,
Saddles all creaking; men complaining,
Chaffing each other as they pass't,
On Ghost Heath turf as they trotted fast.
Now as they neared the Ghost Heath Wood,
Some riders grumbled, "What's the good:
It's shot all day and poached all night.
We shall draw blank and lose the light,
And lose the scent, and lose the day.
Why can't he draw Hope Goneaway,
Or Tuttocks Wood, instead of this?
There's no fox here, there never is."

But as he trotted up to cover,
Robin was watching to discover
What chance there was, and many a token
Told him, that though no hound had spoken,
Most of them stirred to something there.
The old hounds' muzzles searched the air,
Thin ghosts of scents were in their teeth,
From foxes which had crossed the Heath
Not very many hours before.

"We'll find," he said, "I'll bet a score."
Along Ghost Heath they trotted well,
The hoof-cuts made the bruised earth smell,
The shaken brambles scattered drops,
Stray pheasants kukkered out of copse,
Cracking the twigs down with their knockings
And planing out of sight with cockings;
A scut or two lopped white to bramble.

And now they gathered to the gamble
At Ghost Heath Wood on Ghost Heath Down,
The hounds went crackling through the brown
Dry stalks of bracken killed by frost.
The wood stood silent in its host
Of halted trees all winter bare.
The boughs, like veins that suck the air,
Stretched tense, the last leaf scarcely stirred.
There came no song from any bird;
The darkness of the wood stood still
Waiting for fate on Ghost Heath Hill.
The whips crept to the sides to view;
The Master gave the nod, and "Leu,
Leu in, Ed-hoick, Ed-hoick, Leu in,"
Went Robin, cracking through the whin
And through the hedge-gap into cover.
The binders crashed as hounds went over,
And cock-cock-cock the pheasants rose.
Then up went stern and down went nose,
And Robin's cheerful tenor cried,
Through hazel-scrub and stub and ride,
"O wind him beauties, push him out,
Yooi, onto him, Yahout, Yahout,
O push him out, Yooi, wind him, wind him."
The beauties burst the scrub to find him,
They nosed the warren's clipped green lawn,

The bramble and the broom were drawn,
The covert's northern end was blank.

They turned to draw along the bank
Through thicker cover than the Rough
Through three-and-four-year understuff
Where Robin's forearm screened his eyes.
"Yooi, find him, beauties," came his cries.
"Hark, hark to Daffodil," the laughter
Faln from his horn, brought whimpers after,
For ends of scents were everywhere.
He said, "This Hope's a likely lair.
And there's his billets, grey and furred.
And George, he's moving, there's a bird."

A blue uneasy jay was chacking.
(A swearing screech, like tearing sacking)
From tree to tree, as in pursuit,
He said "That's it. There's fox afoot.
And there, they're feathering, there she speaks.
Good Daffodil, good Tarrybreeks,
Hark there, to Daffodil, hark, hark."
The mild horn's note, the soft flaked spark
Of music, fell on that rank scent.
From heart to wild heart magic went.
The whimpering quivered, quavered, rose.
"Daffodil has it. There she goes.
O hark to her." With wild high crying
From frantic hearts, the hounds went flying
To Daffodil for that rank taint.
A waft of it came warm but faint,
In Robin's mouth, and faded so.
"First find a fox, then let him go,"
Cried Robin Dawe. "For any sake.
Ring, Charley, till you're fit to break."

He cheered his beauties like a lover
And charged beside them into cover.

PART II

On old Cold Crendon's windy tops
Grows wintrily Blown Hilcote Copse,
Wind-bitten beech with badger barrows,
Where brocks eat wasp-grubs with their marrows,
And foxes lie on short-grassed turf,
Nose between paws, to hear the surf
Of wind in the beeches drowsily.
There was our fox bred lustily
Three years before, and there he berthed
Under the beech-roots snugly earthed,
With a roof of flint and a floor of chalk
And ten bitten hens' heads each on its stalk,
Some rabbits' paws, some fur from scuts,
A badger's corpse and a smell of guts.
And there on the night before my tale
He trotted out for a point in the vale.
He saw, from the cover edge, the valley
Go trooping down with its droops of sally
To the brimming river's lipping bend,
And a light in the inn at Water's End.
He heard the owl go hunting by
And the shriek of the mouse the owl made die,
And the purr of the owl as he tore the red
Strings from between his claws and fed;
The smack of joy of the horny lips
Marbled green with the blobby strips.
He saw the farms where the dogs were barking,
Cold Crendon Court and Copsecote Larking;
The fault with the spring as bright as gleed,
Green-slash-laced with water weed.

A glare in the sky still marked the town,
Though all folk slept and the blinds were down,
The street lamps watched the empty square,
The night-cat sang his evil there.
The fox's nose tipped up and round
Since smell is a part of sight and sound.
Delicate smells were drifting by,
The sharp nose flaired them heedfully;
Partridges in the clover stubble,
Crouched in a ring for the stoat to nubble.
Rabbit bucks beginning to box;

A scratching place for the pheasant cocks;
A hare in the dead grass near the drain,
And another smell like the spring again.

A faint rank taint like April coming,
It cocked his ears and his blood went drumming,
For somewhere out by Ghost Heath Stubs
Was a roving vixen wanting cubs.
Over the valley, floating faint
On a warmth of windflaw came the taint,
He cocked his ears, he upped his brush,
And he went up wind like an April thrush.
By the Roman Road to Braiches Ridge
Where the fallen willow makes a bridge,
Over the brook by White Hart's Thorn,
To the acres thin with pricking corn.
Over the sparse green hair of the wheat,
By the Clench Brook Mill at Clench Brook Leat,
Through Cowfoot Pastures to Nonely Stevens,
And away to Poltrewood St. Jevons.
Past Tott Hill Down all snaked with meuses,
Past Clench St. Michael and Naunton Crucis,
Past Howle's Oak Farm where the raving brain

Of a dog who heard him foamed his chain,
Then off, as the farmer's window opened,
Past Stonepits Farm to Upton Hope End;
Over short sweet grass and worn flint arrows,
And the three dumb hows of Tencombe Barrows;
And away and away with a rolling scramble,
Through the blackthorn and up the bramble,
With a nose for the smells the night wind carried,
And his red fell clean for being married.
For clicketting time and Ghost Heath Wood
Had put the violet in his blood.

At Tencombe Rings near the Manor Linney,
His foot made the great black stallion whinny,
And the stallion's whinny aroused the stable
And the bloodhound bitches stretched their cable,
And the clink of the bloodhound's chain aroused
The sweet-breathed kye as they chewed and drowsed,
And the stir of the cattle changed the dream
Of the cat in the loft to tense green gleam.
The red-wattled black cock hot from Spain
Crowed from his perch for dawn again,
His breast-pufft hens, one-legged on perch,
Gurgled, beak-down, like men in church,
They crooned in the dark, lifting one red eye
In the raftered roost as the fox went by.

By Tencombe Regis and Slaughters Court,
Through the great grass square of Roman Fort,
By Nun's Wood Yews and the Hungry Hill,
And the Corpse Way Stones all standing still,
By Seven Springs Mead to Deerlip Brook,
And a lolloping leap to Water Hook.
Then with eyes like sparks and his blood awoken
Over the grass to Water's Oaken,

And over the hedge and into ride
In Ghost Heath Wood for his roving bride.

Before the dawn he had loved and fed
And found a kennel and gone to bed
On a shelf of grass in a thick of gorse
That would bleed a hound and blind a horse.
There he slept in the mild west weather
With his nose and brush well tucked together,
He slept like a child, who sleeps yet hears
With the self who needs neither eyes nor ears.

He slept while the pheasant cock untucked
His head from his wing, flew down and kukked,
While the drove of the starlings whirred and wheeled
Out of the ash-trees into field.
While with great black flags that flogged and paddled
The rooks went out to the plough and straddled,
Straddled wide on the moist red cheese,
Of the furrows driven at Uppat's Leas.
Down in the village, men awoke,
The chimneys breathed with a faint blue smoke,
The fox slept on, though tweaks and twitches
Due to his dreams, ran down his flitches.

The cows were milked and the yards were sluict,
And the cocks and hens let out of roost,
Windows were opened, mats were beaten,
All men's breakfasts were cooked and eaten,
But out in the gorse on the grassy shelf,
The sleeping fox looked after himself.

Deep in his dream he heard the life
Of the woodland seek for food or wife,
The hop of a stoat, a buck that thumped,

The squeal of a rat as a weasel jumped,
The blackbird's chackering scattering crying,
The rustling bents from the rabbits flying,
Cows in a byre, and distant men,
And Condicote church-clock striking ten.

At eleven o'clock a boy went past,
With a rough-haired terrier following fast
The boy's sweet whistle and dog's quick yap
Woke the fox from out of his nap.

He rose and stretched till the claws in his pads
Stuck hornily out like long black gads,
He listened a while, and his nose went round
To catch the smell of the distant sound.

The windward smells came free from taint
They were rabbit, strongly, with lime-kiln, faint,
A wild-duck, likely, at Sars Holt Pond,
And sheep on the Sars Holt Down beyond.
The lee-ward smells were much less certain
For the Ghost Heath Hill was like a curtain,
Yet vague, from the lee-ward, now and then,
Came muffled sounds like the sound of men.

He moved to his right to a clearer space,
And all his soul came into his face,
Into his eyes and into his nose,
As over the hill a murmur rose.

His ears were cocked and his keen nose flaired,
He sneered with his lips till his teeth were bared,
He trotted right and lifted a pad
Trying to test what foes he had.

On Ghost Heath turf was a steady drumming
Which sounded like horses quickly coming,

It died as the hunt went down the dip,
Then Malapert yelped at Myngs's whip.
A bright iron horseshoe clinkt on stone,
Then a man's voice spoke, not one alone,
Then a burst of laughter, swiftly still,
Muffled away by Ghost Heath Hill.
Then, indistinctly, the clop, clip, clep,
On Brady Ride, of a horse's step.
Then silence, then, in a burst, much clearer,
Voices and horses coming nearer,
And another noise, of a pit-pat beat
On the Ghost Hill grass, of foxhound feet.

He sat on his haunches listening hard,
While his mind went over the compass card,
Men were coming and rest was done,
But he still had time to get fit to run;
He could outlast horse and outrace hound,
But men were devils from Lobs's Pound.
Scent was burning, the going good
The world one lust for a fox's blood,
The main earths stopped and the drains put-to,
And fifteen miles to the land he knew.
But of all the ills, the ill least pleasant
Was to run in the light when men were present.
Men in the fields to shout and sign
For a lift of hounds to a fox's line.
Men at the earth at the long point's end,
Men at each check and none his friend,
Guessing each shift that a fox contrives,
But still, needs must when the devil drives.

He readied himself, then a soft horn blew,
Then a clear voice carolled "Ed-hoick. Eleu."
Then the wood-end rang with the clear voice crying

And the crackle of scrub where hounds were trying.
Then, the horn blew nearer, a hound's voice quivered,
Then another, then more, till his body shivered,
He left his kennel and trotted thence
With his ears flexed back and his nerves all tense.

He trotted down with his nose intent
For a fox's line to cross his scent,
It was only fair (he being a stranger)
That the native fox should have the danger.
Danger was coming, so swift, so swift,
That the pace of his trot began to lift
The blue-winged Judas, a jay, began
Swearing, hounds whimpered, air stank of man.

He hurried his trotting, he now felt frighted,
It was his poor body made hounds excited
He felt as he ringed the great wood through
That he ought to make for the land he knew.

Then the hounds' excitement quivered and quickened,
Then a horn blew death till his marrow sickened,
Then the wood behind was a crash of cry
For the blood in his veins; it made him fly.

They were on his line; it was death to stay
He must make for home by the shortest way
But with all this yelling and all this wrath
And all these devils, how find a path?

He ran like a stag to the wood's north corner,
Where the hedge was thick and the ditch a yawner,
But the scarlet glimpse of Myngs on Turk,
Watching the woodside, made him shirk.
He ringed the wood and looked at the south.
What wind there was blew into his mouth.

But close to the woodland's blackthorn thicket
Was Dansey, still as a stone, on picket
At Dansey's back were a twenty more
Watching the cover and pressing fore.

The fox drew in and flaired with his muzzle.
Death was there if he messed the puzzle.
There were men without and hounds within,
A crying that stiffened the hair on skin,
Teeth in cover and death without,
Both deaths coming, and no way out.

His nose ranged swiftly, his heart beat fast,
Then a crashing cry rose up in a blast,
Then horse hooves trampled, then horses' flitches
Burst their way through the hazel switches
Then the horn again made the hounds like mad,
And a man, quite near, said "Found, by Gad,"
And a man, quite near, said "Now he'll break.
Lark's Leybourne Copse is the line he'll take."
And the men moved up with their talk and stink
And the traplike noise of the horseshoe clink.
Men whose coming meant death from teeth
In a worrying wrench with him beneath.

The fox sneaked down by the cover side,
(With his ears flexed back) as a snake would glide,
He took the ditch at the cover-end,
He hugged the ditch as his only friend.
The blackbird cock with the golden beak
Got out of his way with a jabbering shriek
And the shriek told Tom on the raking bay
That for eighteen pence he was gone away.

He ran in the hedge in the triple growth
Of bramble and hawthorn, glad of both,

Till a couple of fields were past, and then
Came the living death of the dread of men.

Then, as he listened, he heard a "Hoy,"
Tom Dansey's horn and "Awa-wa-woy."
Then all hounds crying with all their forces,
Then a thundering down of seventy horses.
Robin Dawe's horn and halloos of "Hey
Hark Hollar, Hoik" and "Gone away,"
"Hark Hollar Hoick," and the smack of a whip
A yelp as a tail hound caught the clip.
"Hark Hollar, Hark Hollar"; then Robin made
Pip go crash through the cut-and-laid,
Hounds were over and on his line
With a head like bees upon Tipple Tine.
The sound of the nearness sent a flood
Of terror of death through the fox's blood.
He upped his brush and he cocked his nose,
And he went up wind as a racer goes.

Bold Robin Dawe was over first,
Cheering his hounds on at the burst;
The field were spurring to be in it
"Hold hard, sirs, give them half a minute,"
Came from Sir Peter on his white.
The hounds went romping with delight
Over the grass and got together;
The tail hounds galloped hell-for-leather
After the pack at Myngs's yell;
A cry like every kind of bell
Rang from these rompers as they raced.

The riders thrusting to be placed,
Jammed down their hats and shook their horses,
The hounds romped past with all their forces,

They crashed into the blackthorn fence;
The scent was heavy on their sense,
So hot it seemed the living thing,
It made the blood within them sing,
Gusts of it made their hackles rise,
Hot gulps of it were agonies
Of joy, and thirst for blood, and passion.
"Forrard," cried Robin, "that's the fashion."
He raced beside his pack to cheer.
The field's noise died upon his ear,
A faint horn, far behind, blew thin
In cover, lest some hound were in.
Then instantly the great grass rise
Shut field and cover from his eyes,
He and his racers were alone.
"A dead fox or a broken bone,"
Said Robin, peering for his prey.
The rise, which shut his field away,
Shewed him the vale's great map spread out,
The downs' lean flank and thrusting snout,
Pale pastures, red-brown plough, dark wood,
Blue distance, still as solitude,
Glitter of water here and there,
The trees so delicately bare.
The dark green gorse and bright green holly.
"O glorious God," he said, "how jolly."
And there, down hill, two fields ahead,
The lolloping red dog-fox sped
Over Poor Pastures to the brook.
He grasped these things in one swift look
Then dived into the bulfinch heart
Through thorns that ripped his sleeves apart
And skutched new blood upon his brow.
"His point's Lark's Leybourne Covers now,"
Said Robin, landing with a grunt,

"Forrard, my beautifuls."

　　　　　　　　　The hunt
Followed down hill to race with him,
White Rabbit with his swallow's skim,
Drew within hail, "Quick burst, Sir Peter."
"A traveller.　Nothing could be neater.
Making for Godsdown clumps I take it?"
"Lark's Leybourne, sir, if he can make it.
Forrard."

　　　　　　Bill Ridden thundered down;
His big mouth grinned beneath his frown,
The hounds were going away from horses.
He saw the glint of water-courses,
Yell Brook and Wittold's Dyke ahead,
His horse shoes sliced the green turf red.
Young Cothill's chaser rushed and passt him,
Nob Manor, running next, said "Blast him,
That poet chap who thinks he rides."
Hugh Colway's mare made straking strides
Across the grass, the Colonel next:
Then Squire volleying oaths and vext,
Fighting his hunter for refusing:
Bell Ridden like a cutter cruising
Sailing the grass, then Cob on Warder
Then Minton Price upon Marauder;
Ock Gurney with his eyes intense,
Burning as with a different sense,
His big mouth muttering glad "by damns";
Then Pete crouched down from head to hams,
Rapt like a saint, bright focussed flame.
Bennett with devils in his wame
Chewing black cud and spitting slanting;
Copse scattering jests and Stukely ranting;
Sal Ridden taking line from Dansey;

Long Robert forcing Necromancy;
A dozen more with bad beginnings;
Myngs riding hard to snatch an innings,
A wild last hound with high shrill yelps,
Smacked forrard with some whip-thong skelps.
Then last of all, at top of rise,
The crowd on foot all gasps and eyes
The run up hill had winded them.

They saw the Yell Brook like a gem
Blue in the grass a short mile on
They heard faint cries, but hounds were gone
A good eight fields and out of sight
Except a rippled glimmer white
Going away with dying cheering
And scarlet flappings disappearing,
And scattering horses going, going,
Going like mad, White Rabbit snowing
Far on ahead, a loose horse taking,
Fence after fence with stirrups shaking,
And scarlet specks and dark specks dwindling.

Nearer, were twigs knocked into kindling,
A much bashed fence still dropping stick,
Flung clods, still quivering from the kick,
Cut hoof-marks pale in cheesy clay,
The horse-smell blowing clean away.
Birds flitting back into the cover.
One last faint cry, then all was over.
The hunt had been, and found, and gone.

At Neakings Farm, three furlongs on,
Hounds raced across the Waysmore Road,
Where many of the riders slowed

To tittup down a grassy lane,
Which led as hounds led in the main
And gave no danger of a fall.
There, as they tittupped one and all,
Big Twenty Stone came scattering by,
His great mare made the hoof-casts fly.
"By leave," he cried. "Come on. Come up,
This fox is running like a tup;
Let's leave this lane and get to terms.
No sense in crawling here like worms.
Come let me past and let me start,
This fox is running like a hart,
And this is going to be a run.
Come on. I want to see the fun.
Thanky. By leave. Now, Maiden; do it."
He faced the fence and put her through it
Shielding his eyes lest spikes should blind him,
The crashing blackthorn closed behind him.
Mud-scatters chased him as he scudded.
His mare's ears cocked, her neat feet thudded.

The kestrel cruising over meadow
Watched the hunt gallop on his shadow,
Wee figures, almost at a stand,
Crossing the multi-coloured land,
Slow as a shadow on a dial.

Some horses, swerving at a trial,
Baulked at a fence: at gates they bunched.
The mud about the gates was dunched
Like German cheese; men pushed for places,
And kicked the mud into the faces
Of those who made them room to pass.
The half-mile's gallop on the grass,
Had tailed them out, and warmed their blood.

"His point's the Banner Barton Wood."
"That, or Goat's Gorse."   "A stinger, this."
"You're right in that; by Jove it is."
"An up-wind travelling fox, by George."
"They say Tom viewed him at the forge."
"Well, let me pass and let's be on."

They crossed the lane to Tolderton,
The hill-marl died to valley clay,
And there before them ran the grey
Yell Water, swirling as it ran,
The Yell Brook of the hunting man.
The hunters eyed it and were grim.
They saw the water snaking slim
Ahead, like silver; they could see
(Each man) his pollard willow tree
Firming the bank, they felt their horses
Catch the gleam's hint and gather forces;
They heard the men behind draw near.
Each horse was trembling as a spear
Trembles in hand when tense to hurl,
They saw the brimmed brook's eddies curl.
The willow-roots like water-snakes;
The beaten holes the ratten makes,
They heard the water's rush; they heard
Hugh Colway's mare come like a bird;
A faint cry from the hounds ahead,
Then saddle-strain, the bright hooves' tread,
Quick words, the splash of mud, the launch,
The sick hope that the bank be staunch,
Then Souse, with Souse to left and right.
Maroon across, Sir Peter's white
Down but pulled up, Tom over, Hugh
Mud to the hat but over, too,
Well splashed by Squire who was in.

With draggled pink stuck close to skin,
The Squire leaned from bank and hauled
His mired horse's rein; he bawled
For help from each man racing by.
"What, help you pull him out? Not I.
What made you pull him in?" they said.
Nob Manor cleared and turned his head,
And cried "Wade up. The ford's upstream."
Ock Gurney in a cloud of steam
Stood by his dripping cob and wrung
The taste of brook mud from his tongue
And scraped his poor cob's pasterns clean.
"Lord, what a crowner we've a been,
This jumping brook's a mucky job."
He muttered, grinning, "Lord, poor cob.
Now sir, let me." He turned to Squire
And cleared his hunter from the mire
By skill and sense and strength of arm.

Meanwhile the fox passed Nonesuch Farm,
Keeping the spinney on his right.
Hounds raced him here with all their might
Along the short firm grass, like fire.
The cowman viewed him from the byre
Lolloping on, six fields ahead,
Then hounds, still carrying such a head,
It made him stare, then Rob on Pip,
Sailing the great grass like a ship,
Then grand Maroon in all his glory
Sweeping his strides, his great chest hoary
With foam fleck and the pale hill-marl.
They strode the Leet, they flew the Snarl,
They knocked the nuts at Nonesuch Mill,
Raced up the spur of Gallows Hill
And viewed him there. The line he took

Was Tineton and the Pantry Brook,
Going like fun and hounds like mad.
Tom glanced to see what friends he had
Still within sight, before he turned
The ridge's shoulder; he discerned,
One field away, young Cothill sailing
Easily up. Pete Gurney failing,
Hugh Colway quartering on Sir Peter,
Bill waiting on the mare to beat her,
Sal Ridden skirting to the right.
A horse, with stirrups flashing bright
Over his head at every stride,
Looked like the Major's; Tom espied
Far back, a scarlet speck of man
Running, and straddling as he ran.
Charles Copse was up, Nob Manor followed,
Then Bennett's big-boned black that wallowed
Clumsy, but with the strength of ten.
Then black and brown and scarlet men,
Brown horses, white and black and grey
Scattered a dozen fields away.

The shoulder shut the scene away.
From the Gallows Hill to the Tineton Copse
There were ten ploughed fields like ten full stops,
All wet red clay where a horse's foot
Would be swathed, feet thick, like an ash-tree root.
The fox raced on, on the headlands firm,
Where his swift feet scared the coupling worm,
The rooks rose raving to curse him raw
He snarled a sneer at their swoop and caw.
Then on, then on, down a half ploughed field
Where a ship-like plough drave glitter-keeled,
With a bay horse near and a white horse leading,
And a man saying "Zook" and the red earth bleeding

He gasped as he saw the ploughman drop
The stilts and swear at the team to stop.
The ploughman ran in his red clay clogs
Crying "Zick un Towzer; zick, good dogs."
A couple of wire-haired lurchers lean
Arose from his wallet, nosing keen;
With a rushing swoop they were on his track,
Putting chest to stubble to bite his back.
He swerved from his line with the curs at heel,
The teeth as they missed him clicked like steel,
With a worrying snarl, they quartered on him,
While the ploughman shouted "Zick; upon him."

The lurcher dogs soon shot their bolt,
And the fox raced on by the Hazel Holt,
Down the dead grass tilt to the sandstone gash
Of the Pantry Brook at Tineton Ash.
The loitering water, flooded full,
Had yeast on its lip like raddled wool,
It was wrinkled over with Arab script
Of eddies that twisted up and slipt.
The stepping stones had a rush about them
So the fox plunged in and swam without them.

He crossed to the cattle's drinking shallow
Firmed up with rush and the roots of mallow,
He wrung his coat from his draggled bones
And romped away for the Sarsen Stones.

A sneaking glance with his ears flexed back,
Made sure that his scent had failed the pack,
For the red clay, good for corn and roses,
Was cold for scent and brought hounds to noses.
He slackened pace by the Tineton Tree,
(A vast hollow ash-tree grown in three),

He wriggled a shake and padded slow,
Not sure if the hounds were on or no.

A horn blew faint, then he heard the sounds
Of a cantering huntsman, lifting hounds,
The ploughman had raised his hat for sign,
And the hounds were lifted and on his line.
He heard the splash in the Pantry Brook,
And a man's voice: "Thiccy's the line he took,"
And a clear "Yoi doit" and a whimpering quaver,
Though the lurcher dogs had dulled the savour.

The fox went off while the hounds made halt,
And the horses breathed and the field found fault,
But the whimpering rose to a crying crash
By the hollow ruin of Tineton Ash.
Then again the kettle drum horse hooves beat,
And the green blades bent to the fox's feet
And the cry rose keen not far behind
Of the "Blood, blood, blood" in the fox-hounds' mind.

The fox was strong, he was full of running,
He could run for an hour and then be cunning,
But the cry behind him made him chill,
They were nearer now and they meant to kill.
They meant to run him until his blood
Clogged on his heart as his brush with mud,
Till his back bent up and his tongue hung flagging,
And his belly and brush were filthed from dragging.
Till he crouched stone still, dead-beat and dirty,
With nothing but teeth against the thirty.
And all the way to that blinding end
He would meet with men and have none his friend.
Men to holloa and men to run him,
With stones to stagger and yells to stun him,

Men to head him, with whips to beat him,
Teeth to mangle and mouths to eat him.
And all the way, that wild high crying,
To cold his blood with the thought of dying,
The horn and the cheer, and the drum-like thunder,
Of the horse hooves stamping the meadows under.
He upped his brush and went with a will
For the Sarsen Stones on Wan Dyke Hill.

As he ran the meadow by Tineton Church,
A christening party left the porch,
They stood stock still as he pounded by,
They wished him luck but they thought he'd die.
The toothless babe in his long white coat
Looked delicate meat, the fox took note;
But the sight of them grinning there, pointing finger,
Made him put on steam till he went a stinger.

Past Tineton Church over Tineton Waste,
With the lolloping ease of a fox's haste,
The fur on his chest blown dry with the air,
His brush still up and his cheek-teeth bare.
Over the Waste where the ganders grazed,
The long swift lilt of his loping lazed,
His ears cocked up as his blood ran higher,
He saw his point, and his eyes took fire.
The Wan Dyke Hill with its fir tree barren,
Its dark of gorse and its rabbit warren.
The Dyke on its heave like a tightened girth,
And holes in the Dyke where a fox might earth.
He had rabbitted there long months before,
The earths were deep and his need was sore,
The way was new, but he took a bearing,
And rushed like a blown ship billow-sharing.

Off Tineton Common to Tineton Dean,
Where the wind-hid elders pushed with green:
Through the Dean's thin cover across the lane,
And up Midwinter to King of Spain.
Old Joe at digging his garden grounds,
Said "A fox, being hunted; where be hounds?
O lord, my back, to be young again,
'Stead a zellin zider in King of Spain.
O hark, I hear 'em, O sweet, O sweet.
Why there be redcoat in Gearge's wheat.
And there be redcoat, and there they gallop.
Thur go a browncoat down a wallop.
Quick, Ellen, quick, come Susan, fly.
Here'm hounds. I zeed the fox go by,
Go by like thunder, go by like blasting,
With his girt white teeth all looking ghasting.
Look there come hounds. Hark, hear 'em crying,
Lord, belly to stubble, ain't they flying.
There's huntsmen, there. The fox come past,
(As I was digging) as fast as fast.
He's only been gone a minute by;
A girt dark dog as pert as pye."

Ellen and Susan came out scattering
Brooms and dustpans till all was clattering;
They saw the pack come head to foot
Running like racers nearly mute;
Robin and Dansey quartering near,
All going gallop like startled deer.
A half dozen flitting scarlets shewing
In the thin green Dean where the pines were growing.
Black coats and brown coats thrusting and spurring
Sending the partridge coveys whirring,
Then a rattle up hill and a clop up lane,
It emptied the bar of the King of Spain.

Tom left his cider, Dick left his bitter,
Granfer James left his pipe and spitter,
Out they came from the sawdust floor,
They said, "They'm going." They said "O Lor."

The fox raced on, up the Barton Balks,
With a crackle of kex in the nettle stalks,
Over Hammond's grass to the dark green line
Of the larch-wood smelling of turpentine.
Scratch Steven Larches, black to the sky,
A sadness breathing with one long sigh,
Grey ghosts of trees under funeral plumes,
A mist of twig over soft brown glooms.
As he entered the wood he heard the smacks,
Chip-jar, of the fir pole feller's axe,
He swerved to the left to a broad green ride,
Where a boy made him rush for the further side.
He swerved to the left, to the Barton Road,
But there were the timberers come to load.
Two timber carts and a couple of carters
With straps round their knees instead of garters.
He swerved to the right, straight down the wood,
The carters watched him, the boy hallooed.
He leaped from the larch-wood into tillage,
The cobbler's garden of Barton village.

The cobbler bent at his wooden foot,
Beating sprigs in a broken boot;
He wore old glasses with thick horn rim,
He scowled at his work for his sight was dim.
His face was dingy, his lips were grey,
From primming sparrowbills day by day;
As he turned his boot he heard a noise
At his garden-end and he thought, "It's boys."

He saw his cat nip up on the shed,
Where her back arched up till it touched her head,
He saw his rabbit race round and round
Its little black box three feet from ground.
His six hens cluckered and flucked to perch,
"That's boys," said cobbler, "so I'll go search."
He reached his stick and blinked in his wrath,
When he saw a fox in his garden path.
The fox swerved left and scrambled out
Knocking crinked green shells from the Brussels Sprout,
He scrambled out through the cobbler's paling,
And up Pill's orchard to Purton's Tailing,
Across the plough at the top of bent,
Through the heaped manure to kill his scent,
Over to Aldams, up to Cappells,
Past Nursery Lot with its white-washed apples,
Past Colston's Broom, past Gaunts, past Sheres,
Past Foxwhelps Oasts with their hooded ears,
Past Monk's Ash Clerewell, past Beggars Oak,
Past the great elms blue with the Hinton smoke,
Along Long Hinton to Hinton Green,
Where the wind-washed steeple stood serene
With its golden bird still sailing air,
Past Banner Barton, past Chipping Bare,
Past Maddings Hollow, down Dundry Dip,
And up Goose Grass to the Sailing Ship.

The three black firs of the Ship stood still
On the bare chalk heave of the Dundry Hill,
The fox looked back as he slackened past
The scaled red-bole of the mizzen-mast.

There they were coming, mute but swift,
A scarlet smear in the blackthorn rift,
A white horse rising, a dark horse flying,

And the hungry hounds too tense for crying.
Stormcock leading, his stern spear-straight,
Racing as though for a piece of plate,
Little speck horsemen field on field;
Then Dansey viewed him and Robin squealed.

At the View Halloo the hounds went frantic,
Back went Stormcock and up went Antic,
Up went Skylark as Antic sped
It was zest to blood how they carried head.
Skylark drooped as Maroon drew by,
Their hackles lifted, they scored to cry.

The fox knew well, that before they tore him,
They should try their speed on the downs before him,
There were three more miles to the Wan Dyke Hill,
But his heart was high, that he beat them still.
The wind of the downland charmed his bones
So off he went for the Sarsen Stones.

The moan of the three great firs in the wind,
And the Ai of the foxhounds died behind,
Wind-dapples followed the hill-wind's breath
On the Kill Down gorge where the Danes found death;
Larks scattered up; the peewits feeding
Rose in a flock from the Kill Down Steeding.
The hare leaped up from her form and swerved
Swift left for the Starveall harebell-turved.
On the wind-bare thorn some longtails prinking
Cried sweet, as though wind blown glass were chinking.
Behind came thudding and loud halloo
Or a cry from hounds as they came to view.

The pure clean air came sweet to his lungs,
Till he thought foul scorn of those crying tongues,

In a three mile more he would reach the haven
In the Wan Dyke croaked on by the raven,
In a three mile more he would make his berth
On the hard cool floor of a Wan Dyke earth,
Too deep for spade, too curved for terrier,
With the pride of the race to make rest the merrier.
In a three mile more he would reach his dream,
So his game heart gulped and he put on steam.

Like a rocket shot to a ship ashore,
The lean red bolt of his body tore,
Like a ripple of wind running swift on grass,
Like a shadow on wheat when a cloud blows past,
Like a turn at the buoy in a cutter sailing,
When the bright green gleam lips white at the railing,
Like the April snake whipping back to sheath,
Like the gannet's hurtle on fish beneath,
Like a kestrel chasing, like a sickle reaping,
Like all things swooping, like all things sweeping,
Like a hound for stay, like a stag for swift,
With his shadow beside like spinning drift.

Past the gibbet-stock all stuck with nails,
Where they hanged in chains what had hung at jails,
Past Ashmundshowe where Ashmund sleeps,
And none but the tumbling peewit weeps,
Past Curlew Calling, the gaunt grey corner
Where the curlew comes as a summer mourner,
Past Blowbury Beacon shaking his fleece,
Where all winds hurry and none brings peace,
Then down, on the mile-long green decline
Where the turf's like spring and the air's like wine,
Where the sweeping spurs of the downland spill
Into Wan Brook Valley and Wan Dyke Hill.
On he went with a galloping rally

Past Maesbury Clump for Wan Brook Valley,
The blood in his veins went romping high
"Get on, on, on to the earth or die."
The air of the downs went purely past,
Till he felt the glory of going fast,
Till the terror of death, though there indeed,
Was lulled for a while by his pride of speed;
He was romping away from hounds and hunt,
He had Wan Dyke Hill and his earth in front,
In a one mile more when his point was made,
He would rest in safety from dog or spade;
Nose between paws he would hear the shout
Of the "gone to earth" to the hounds without,
The whine of the hounds, and their cat feet gadding,
Scratching the earth, and their breath pad-padding,
He would hear the horn call hounds away,
And rest in peace till another day.
In one mile more he would lie at rest
So for one mile more he would go his best.
He reached the dip at the long droop's end
And he took what speed he had still to spend.

So down past Maesbury beech clump grey,
That would not be green till the end of May,
Past Arthur's Table, the white chalk boulder,
Where pasque flowers purple the down's grey shoulder
Past Quichelm's Keeping, past Harry's Thorn
To Thirty Acre all thin with corn.
As he raced the corn towards Wan Dyke Brook,
The pack had view of the way he took,
Robin hallooed from the downland's crest,
He capped them on till they did their best.
The quarter mile to the Wan Brook's brink
Was raced as quick as a man can think.
And here, as he ran to the huntsman's yelling,

The fox first felt that the pace was telling,
His body and lungs seemed all grown old,
His legs less certain, his heart less bold,
The hound-noise nearer, the hill slope steeper,
The thud in the blood of his body deeper,
His pride in his speed, his joy in the race
Were withered away, for what use was pace?
He had run his best, and the hounds ran better.
Then the going worsened, the earth was wetter.
Then his brush drooped down till it sometimes dragged,
And his fur felt sick and his chest was tagged
With taggles of mud, and his pads seemed lead,
It was well for him he'd an earth ahead.
Down he went to the brook and over,
Out of the corn and into the clover,
Over the slope that the Wan Brook drains,
Past Battle Tump where they earthed the Danes,
Then up the hill that the Wan Dyke rings
Where the Sarsen Stones stand grand like kings.

Seven Sarsens of granite grim,
As he ran them by they looked at him;
As he leaped the lip of their earthen paling
The hounds were gaining and he was failing.

He passed the Sarsens, he left the spur,
He pressed up hill to the blasted fir,
He slipped as he leaped the hedge; he slithered;
"He's mine," thought Robin. "He's done; he's dithered."
At the second attempt he cleared the fence,
He turned half right where the gorse was dense,
He was leading hounds by a furlong clear.
He was past his best, but his earth was near.
He ran up gorse, to the spring of the ramp,
The steep green wall of the dead men's camp,

He sidled up it and scampered down
To the deep green ditch of the dead men's town.

Within, as he reached that soft green turf,
The wind, blowing lonely, moaned like surf,
Desolate ramparts rose up steep,
On either side, for the ghosts to keep.
He raced the trench, past the rabbit warren,
Close grown with moss which the wind made barren,
He passed the spring where the rushes spread,
And there in the stones was his earth ahead.
One last short burst upon failing feet,
There life lay waiting, so sweet, so sweet,
Rest in a darkness, balm for aches.

The earth was stopped.   It was barred with stakes.

With the hounds at head so close behind
He had to run as he changed his mind.
This earth, as he saw, was stopped, but still
There was one earth more on the Wan Dyke Hill.
A rabbit burrow a furlong on,
He could kennel there till the hounds were gone.
Though his death seemed near he did not blench
He upped his brush and ran the trench.

He ran the trench while the wind moaned treble,
Earth trickled down, there were falls of pebble.
Down in the valley of that dark gash
The wind-withered grasses looked like ash.
Trickles of stones and earth fell down
In that dark valley of dead men's town.
A hawk arose from a fluff of feathers,
From a distant fold came a bleat of wethers.

He heard no noise from the hounds behind
But the hill-wind moaning like something blind.

He turned the bend in the hill and there
Was his rabbit-hole with its mouth worn bare,
But there with a gun tucked under his arm
Was young Sid Kissop of Purlpits Farm,
With a white hob ferret to drive the rabbit
Into a net which was set to nab it.
And young Jack Cole peered over the wall
And loosed a pup with a "Z'bite en, Saul,"
The terrier pup attacked with a will,
So the fox swerved right and away down hill.

Down from the ramp of the Dyke he ran
To the brackeny patch where the gorse began,
Into the gorse, where the hill's heave hid
The line he took from the eyes of Sid
He swerved down wind and ran like a hare
For the wind-blown spinney below him there.

He slipped from the gorse to the spinney dark
(There were curled grey growths on the oak tree bark)
He saw no more of the terrier pup.
But he heard men speak and the hounds come up.

He crossed the spinney with ears intent
For the cry of hounds on the way he went
His heart was thumping, the hounds were near now
He could make no sprint at a cry and cheer now,
He was past his perfect, his strength was failing,
His brush sag-sagged and his legs were ailing.
He felt as he skirted Dead Men's Town,
That in one mile more they would have him down.

Through the withered oak's wind-crouching tops
He saw men's scarlet above the copse,
He heard men's oaths, yet he felt hounds slacken
In the frondless stalks of the brittle bracken.
He felt that the unseen link which bound
His spine to the nose of the leading hound,
Was snapped, that the hounds no longer knew
Which way to follow nor what to do;
That the threat of the hound's teeth left his neck,
They had ceased to run, they had come to check,
They were quartering wide on the Wan Hill's bent.

The terrier's chase had killed his scent.

He heard bits chink as the horses shifted,
He heard hounds cast, then he heard hounds lifted,
But there came no cry from a new attack,
His heart grew steady, his breath came back.

He left the spinney and ran its edge,
By the deep dry ditch of the blackthorn hedge,
Then out of the ditch and down the meadow,
Trotting at ease in the blackthorn shadow
Over the track called Godsdown Road,
To the great grass heave of the gods' abode,
He was moving now upon land he knew
Up Clench Royal and Morton Tew
The Pol Brook, Cheddesdon and East Stoke Church,
High Clench St. Lawrence and Tinker's Birch,
Land he had roved on night by night,
For hot blood suckage or furry bite,
The threat of the hounds behind was gone;
He breathed deep pleasure and trotted on.

While young Sid Kissop thrashed the pup,
Robin on Pip came heaving up,

And found his pack spread out at check.
"I'd like to wring your terrier's neck,"
He said, "You see? He's spoiled our sport.
He's killed the scent." He broke off short,
And stared at hounds and at the valley.
No jay or magpie gave a rally
Down in the copse, no circling rooks
Rose over fields; old Joyful's looks
Were doubtful in the gorse, the pack
Quested both up and down and back.
He watched each hound for each small sign.
They tried, but could not hit the line,
The scent was gone. The field took place
Out of the way of hounds. The pace
Had tailed them out; though four remained:
Sir Peter, on White Rabbit stained
Red from the brooks, Bill Ridden cheery,
Hugh Colway with his mare dead weary.
The Colonel with Marauder beat.
They turned towards a thud of feet;
Dansey, and then young Cothill came
(His chestnut mare was galloped tame).
"There's Copse, a field behind," he said.
"Those last miles put them all to bed.
They're strung along the downs like flies."
Copse and Nob Manor topped the rise.
"Thank God, a check," they said, "at last."

"They cannot own it; you must cast,"
Sir Peter said. The soft horn blew
Tom turned the hounds up wind; they drew
Up wind, down hill, by spinney side.
They tried the brambled ditch; they tried
The swamp, all choked with bright green grass
And clumps of rush and pools like glass,

Long since, the dead men's drinking pond.
They tried the White Leaved Oak beyond,
But no hound spoke to it or feathered.
The horse heads drooped like horses tethered,
The men mopped brows. "An hour's hard run.
Ten miles," they said, "we must have done.
It's all of six from Colston's Gorses."
The lucky got their second horses.

The time ticked by. "He's lost," they muttered.
A pheasant rose. A rabbit scuttered.
Men mopped their scarlet cheeks and drank.

They drew down wind along the bank,
(The Wan Way) on the hill's south spur,
Grown with dwarf oak and juniper
Like dwarves alive, but no hound spoke.
The seepings made the ground one soak.
They turned the spur; the hounds were beat.
Then Robin shifted in his seat
Watching for signs, but no signs shewed.
"I'll lift across the Godsdown Road,
Beyond the spinney," Robin said.
Tom turned them; Robin went ahead.

Beyond the copse a great grass fallow
Stretched towards Stoke and Cheddesdon Mallow,
A rolling grass where hounds grew keen.
"Yoi doit, then; this is where he's been,"
Said Robin, eager at their joy.
"Yooi, Joyful, lad, yooi, Cornerboy.
  They're on to him."
                              At his reminders
The keen hounds hurried to the finders.
The finding hounds began to hurry,

Men jammed their hats prepared to skurry,
The Ai Ai of the cry began.
Its spirit passed to horse and man,
The skirting hounds romped to the cry.
Hound after hound cried Ai Ai Ai,
Till all were crying, running, closing,
Their heads well up and no heads nosing,
Joyful ahead with spear-straight stern.
They raced the great slope to the burn.
Robin beside them, Tom behind,
Pointing past Robin down the wind.

For there, two furlongs on, he viewed
On Holy Hill or Cheddesdon Rood
Just where the ploughland joined the grass,
A speck down the first furrow pass,
A speck the colour of the plough.
"Yonder he goes. We'll have him now,"
He cried. The speck passed slowly on,
It reached the ditch, paused, and was gone.

Then down the slope and up the Rood,
Went the hunt's gallop. Godsdown Wood
Dropped its last oak-leaves at the rally.
Over the Rood to High Clench Valley
The gallop led; the red-coats scattered,
The fragments of the hunt were tattered
Over five fields, ev'n since the check.
"A dead fox or a broken neck,"
Said Robin Dawe, "Come up, the Dane."
The hunter leant against the rein,
Cocking his ears, he loved to see
The hounds at cry. The hounds and he
The chiefs in all that feast of pace.

The speck in front began to race.

The fox heard hounds get on to his line,
And again the terror went down his spine,
Again the back of his neck felt cold,
From the sense of the hound's teeth taking hold.
But his legs were rested, his heart was good,
He had breath to gallop to Mourne End Wood,
It was four miles more, but an earth at end,
So he put on pace down the Rood Hill Bend.

Down the great grass slope which the oak trees dot
With a swerve to the right from the keeper's cot,
Over High Clench brook in its channel deep,
To the grass beyond, where he ran to sheep.
The sheep formed line like a troop of horse,
They swerved, as he passed, to front his course
From behind, as he ran, a cry arose,
"See the sheep, there.   Watch them.   There he goes."

He ran the sheep that their smell might check
The hounds from his scent and save his neck,
But in two fields more he was made aware
That the hounds still ran; Tom had viewed him there.

Tom had held them on through the taint of sheep,
They had kept his line, as they meant to keep,
They were running hard with a burning scent,
And Robin could see which way he went.
The pace that he went brought strain to breath,
He knew as he ran that the grass was death.
He ran the slope towards Morton Tew
That the heave of the hill might stop the view,
Then he doubled down to the Blood Brook red,
And swerved upstream in the brook's deep bed.
He splashed the shallows, he swam the deeps,
He crept by banks as a moorhen creeps,

He heard the hounds shoot over his line,
And go on, on, on towards Cheddesdon Zine.

In the minute's peace he could slacken speed,
The ease from the strain was sweet indeed.
Cool to the pads the water flowed,
He reached the bridge on the Cheddesdon road.

As he came to light from the culvert dim,
Two boys on the bridge looked down on him;
They were young Bill Ripple and Harry Meun,
"Look, there be squirrel, a-swimmin', see 'un."
"Noa, ben't a squirrel, be fox, be fox.
Now, Hal, get pebble, we'll give en socks."
"Get pebble, Billy, dub un a plaster;
There's for thy belly, I'll learn ee, master."

The stones splashed spray in the fox's eyes,
He raced from brook in a burst of shies,
He ran for the reeds in the withy car,
Where the dead flags shake and the wild-duck are.

He pushed through the reeds which cracked at his passing,
To the High Clench Water, a grey pool glassing,
He heard Bill Ripple in Cheddesdon road,
Shout, "This way, huntsman, it's here he goed."

The Leu Leu Leu went the soft horn's laughter,
The hounds (they had checked) came romping after,
The clop of the hooves on the road was plain,
Then the crackle of reeds, then cries again.

A whimpering first, then Robin's cheer,
Then the Ai Ai Ai; they were all too near;

His swerve had brought but a minute's rest
Now he ran again, and he ran his best.

With a crackle of dead dry stalks of reed
The hounds came romping at topmost speed
The redcoats ducked as the great hooves skittered
The Blood Brook's shallows to sheets that glittered;
With a cracking whip and a "Hoik, Hoik, Hoik,
Forrard," Tom galloped. Bob shouted "Yoick."
Like a running fire the dead reeds crackled
The hounds' heads lifted, their necks were hackled.
Tom cried to Bob as they thundered through,
"He is running short, we shall kill at Tew."
Bob cried to Tom as they rode in team,
"I was sure, that time, that he turned upstream.
As the hounds went over the brook in stride,
I saw old Daffodil fling to side,
So I guessed at once, when they checked beyond."
The ducks flew up from the Morton Pond.
The fox looked up at their tailing strings,
He wished (perhaps) that a fox had wings.
Wings with his friends in a great V straining
The autumn sky when the moon is gaining;
For better the grey sky's solitude,
Than to be two miles from the Mourne End Wood
With the hounds behind, clean-trained to run,
And your strength half spent and your breath half done.
Better the reeds and the sky and water
Than that hopeless pad from a certain slaughter.
At the Morton Pond the fields began,
Long Tew's green meadows; he ran; he ran.

First the six green fields that make a mile,
With the lip-full Clench at the side the while,
With the rooks above, slow-circling, shewing

The world of men where a fox was going;
The fields all empty, dead grass, bare hedges,
And the brook's bright gleam in the dark of sedges.
To all things else he was dumb and blind,
He ran, with the hounds a field behind.

At the sixth green field came the long slow climb,
To the Mourne End Wood as old as time
Yew woods dark, where they cut for bows,
Oak woods green with the mistletoes,
Dark woods evil, but burrowed deep
With a brock's earth strong, where a fox might sleep.
He saw his point on the heaving hill,
He had failing flesh and a reeling will,
He felt the heave of the hill grow stiff,
He saw black woods, which would shelter—If—
Nothing else, but the steepening slope,
And a black line nodding, a line of hope
The line of the yews on the long slope's brow,
A mile, three-quarters, a half-mile now.
A quarter-mile, but the hounds had viewed
They yelled to have him this side the wood,
Robin capped them, Tom Dansey steered them
With a "Yooi, Yooi, Yooi," Bill Ridden cheered them.
Then up went hackles as Shatterer led,
"Mob him," cried Ridden, "the wood's ahead.
Turn him, damn it; Yooi, beauties, beat him,
O God, let them get him; let them eat him.
O God," said Ridden, "I'll eat him stewed,
If you'll let us get him this side the wood."

But the pace, uphill, made a horse like stone,
The pack went wild up the hill alone.
Three hundred yards, and the worst was past,
The slope was gentler and shorter-grassed,

The fox saw the bulk of the woods grow tall
On the brae ahead like a barrier-wall.
He saw the skeleton trees show sky,
And the yew trees darken to see him die
And the line of the woods go reeling black
There was hope in the woods, and behind, the pack.

Two hundred yards, and the trees grew taller,
Blacker, blinder, as hope grew smaller
Cry seemed nearer, the teeth seemed gripping
Pulling him back, his pads seemed slipping.
He was all one ache, one gasp, one thirsting,
Heart on his chest-bones, beating, bursting
The hounds were gaining like spotted pards
And the wood-hedge still was a hundred yards.
The wood-hedge black was a two year, quick
Cut-and-laid that had sprouted thick
Thorns all over, and strongly plied,
With a clean red ditch on the take-off side.

He saw it now as a redness, topped
With a wattle of thorn-work spiky cropped,
Spiky to leap on, stiff to force,
No safe jump for a failing horse,
But beyond it, darkness of yews together,
Dark green plumes over soft brown feather,
Darkness of woods where scents were blowing
Strange scents, hot scents, of wild things going,
Scents that might draw these hounds away.
So he ran, ran, ran to that clean red clay.

Still, as he ran, his pads slipped back,
All his strength seemed to draw the pack,
The trees drew over him dark like Norns,
He was over the ditch and at the thorns.

He thrust at the thorns, which would not yield,
He leaped, but fell, in sight of the field,
The hounds went wild as they saw him fall,
The fence stood stiff like a Bucks flint wall.

He gathered himself for a new attempt,
His life before was an old dream dreamt,
All that he was was a blown fox quaking,
Jumping at thorns too stiff for breaking,
While over the grass in crowd, in cry,
Came the grip teeth grinning to make him die,
The eyes intense, dull, smouldering red,
The fell like a ruff round each keen head
The pace like fire, and scarlet men
Galloping, yelling, "Yooi, eat him, then."
He gathered himself, he leaped, he reached
The top of the hedge like a fish-boat beached
He steadied a second and then leaped down
To the dark of the wood where bright things drown.

He swerved, sharp right, under young green firs.
Robin called on the Dane with spurs,
He cried "Come, Dansey: if God's not good,
We shall change our fox in this Mourne End Wood."
Tom cried back as he charged like spate,
"Mine can't jump that, I must ride to gate."
Robin answered, "I'm going at him.
I'll kill that fox, if he kills me, drat him.
We'll kill in covert. Gerr on, now, Dane."
He gripped him tight and he made it plain,
He slowed him down till he almost stood
While his hounds went crash into Mourne End Wood.

Like a dainty dancer with footing nice,
The Dane turned side for a leap in twice.

He cleared the ditch to the red clay bank,
He rose at the fence as his quarters sank,
He barged the fence as the bank gave way
And down he came in a fall of clay.

Robin jumped off him and gasped for breath;
He said "That's lost him as sure as death.
They've over-run him. Come up, the Dane,
But I'll kill him yet, if we ride to Spain."

He scrambled up to his horse's back,
He thrust through cover, he called his pack,
He cheered them on till they made it good,
Where the fox had swerved inside the wood.

The fox knew well as he ran the dark,
That the headlong hounds were past their mark
They had missed his swerve and had overrun.
But their devilish play was not yet done.

For a minute he ran and heard no sound,
Then a whimper came from a questing hound,
Then a "This way, beauties," and then "Leu Leu,"
The floating laugh of the horn that blew.
Then the cry again and the crash and rattle
Of the shrubs burst back as they ran to battle.
Till the wood behind seemed risen from root,
Crying and crashing to give pursuit,
Till the trees seemed hounds and the air seemed cry,
And the earth so far that he needs but die,
Die where he reeled in the woodland dim
With a hound's white grips in the spine of him;
For one more burst he could spurt, and then
Wait for the teeth, and the wrench, and men.

He made his spurt for the Mourne End rocks,
The air blew rank with the taint of fox;
The yews gave way to a greener space
Of great stones strewn in a grassy place.
And there was his earth at the great grey shoulder,
Sunk in the ground, of a granite boulder
A dry deep burrow with rocky roof,
Proof against crowbars, terrier-proof,
Life to the dying, rest for bones.

The earth was stopped; it was filled with stones.

Then, for a moment, his courage failed,
His eyes looked up as his body quailed,
Then the coming of death, which all things dread,
Made him run for the wood ahead.

The taint of fox was rank on the air,
He knew, as he ran, there were foxes there.
His strength was broken, his heart was bursting
His bones were rotten, his throat was thirsting
His feet were reeling, his brush was thick
From dragging the mud, and his brain was sick.

He thought as he ran of his old delight
In the wood in the moon in an April night,
His happy hunting, his winter loving,
The smells of things in the midnight roving;
The look of his dainty-nosing, red
Clean-felled dam with her footpad's tread,
Of his sire, so swift, so game, so cunning
With craft in his brain and power of running,
Their fights of old when his teeth drew blood.
Now he was sick, with his coat all mud.

He crossed the covert, he crawled the bank,
To a meuse in the thorns and there he sank,
With his ears flexed back and his teeth shown white,
In a rat's resolve for a dying bite.

And there, as he lay, he saw the vale,
That a struggling sunlight silvered pale,
The Deerlip Brook like a strip of steel,
The Nun's Wood Yews where the rabbits squeal,
The great grass square of the Roman Fort,
And the smoke in the elms at Crendon Court.

And above the smoke in the elm-tree tops,
Was the beech-clump's blue, Blown Hilcote Copse,
Where he and his mates had long made merry
In the bloody joys of the rabbit-herry.

And there as he lay and looked, the cry
Of the hounds at head came rousing by;
He bent his bones in the blackthorn dim.

But the cry of the hounds was not for him
Over the fence with a crash they went,
Belly to grass, with a burning scent,
Then came Dansey, yelling to Bob,
"They've changed, O damn it, now here's a job."
And Bob yelled back, "Well, we cannot turn 'em,
It's Jumper and Antic, Tom; we'll learn 'em.
We must just go on, and I hope we kill."
They followed hounds down the Mourne End Hill.
The fox lay still in the rabbit-meuse,
On the dry brown dust of the plumes of yews.
In the bottom below a brook went by,
Blue, in a patch, like a streak of sky.
There, one by one, with a clink of stone

Came a red or dark coat on a horse half blown.
And man to man with a gasp for breath
Said, "Lord, what a run. I'm fagged to death."

After an hour, no riders came,
The day drew by like an ending game;
A robin sang from a pufft red breast,
The fox lay quiet and took his rest.
A wren on a tree-stump carolled clear,
Then the starlings wheeled in a sudden sheer,
The rooks came home to the twiggy hive
In the elm-tree tops which the winds do drive.
Then the noise of the rooks fell slowly still,
And the lights came out in the Clench Brook Mill
Then a pheasant cocked, then an owl began
With the cry that curdles the blood of man.

The stars grew bright as the yews grew black,
The fox rose stiffly and stretched his back.
He flaired the air, then he padded out
To the valley below him dark as doubt,
Winter-thin with the young green crops,
For Old Cold Crendon and Hilcote Copse.

As he crossed the meadows at Naunton Larking,
The dogs in the town all started barking,
For with feet all bloody and flanks all foam,
The hounds and the hunt were limping home;
Limping home in the dark, dead-beaten,
The hounds all rank from a fox they'd eaten,
Dansey saying to Robin Dawe,
"The fastest and longest I ever saw."
And Robin answered, "O Tom, 'twas good,
I thought they'd changed in the Mourne End Wood,
But now I feel that they did not change.

We've had a run that was great and strange;
And to kill in the end, at dusk, on grass.
We'll turn to the Cock and take a glass,
For the hounds, poor souls, are past their forces.
And a gallon of ale for our poor horses,
And some bits of bread for the hounds, poor things,
After all they've done (for they've done like kings),
Would keep them going till we get in.
We had it alone from Nun's Wood Whin."
Then Tom replied, "If they changed or not,
There've been few runs longer and none more hot,
We shall talk of to-day until we die."

The stars grew bright in the winter sky,
The wind came keen with a tang of frost,
The brook was troubled for new things lost,
The copse was happy for old things found,
The fox came home and he went to ground.

And the hunt came home and the hounds were fed,
They climbed to their bench and went to bed,
The horses in stable loved their straw.
"Good-night, my beauties," said Robin Dawe.

Then the moon came quiet and flooded full
Light and beauty on clouds like wool,
On a feasted fox at rest from hunting,
In the beech wood grey where the brocks were grunting.

The beech wood grey rose dim in the night
With moonlight fallen in pools of light,
The long dead leaves on the ground were rimed.
A clock struck twelve and the church-bells chimed.

ENSLAVED

ALL early in the April when daylight comes at five
I went into the garden most glad to be alive
The thrushes and the blackbirds were singing in the thorn
The April flowers were singing for joy of being born.

I smelt the dewy morning come blowing through the woods
Where all the wilding cherries do toss their snowy snoods
I thought of the running water where sweet white violets grow
I said, "I'll pick them for her, because she loves them so."

So in the dewy morning I turned to climb the hill
Beside the running water whose tongue is never still,
O delicate green and dewy were all the budding trees
The blue dog-violets grew there and many primroses.

Out of the wood I wandered, but paused upon the heath
To watch, beyond the tree tops, the wrinkled sea beneath
Its blueness and its stillness were trembling as it lay
In the old un-autumned beauty that never goes away.

And the beauty of the water brought my love into my mind
Because all sweet love is beauty and the loved thing turns
     to kind
And I thought, "It is a beauty spread, for setting of your grace,
O white violet of a woman with the April in your face."

So I gathered the white violets where young men pick them
     still,
And I turned to cross the woodland to her house beneath the
     hill,

And I thought of her delight in the flowers that I brought her,
Bright like sunlight, sweet like singing, cool like running of the
water.

Now I noticed as I crossed the wood towards my lady's house,
That wisps of smoke were blowing blue in the young green of the
boughs:
But I thought, "They're burning weeds," and I felt the green
and blue
To be lovely, so, together, while the green was in its dew.

Then I smelt the smell of burning; but I thought, "The bonfire
takes,
And the tongues of flame are licking up below the lifting flakes."
Though, I thought, "the fire must be big, to raise a smoke so
thick."
And I wondered for a moment if the fire were a rick.

But the love that sang within me made me put the thought
away,
What do young men care for trouble if they see their love to-day,
And my thought kept running forward till it knelt before my
sweet,
Laying thought and joy and service in a love-gift at her feet.

And I thought of life beside her, and of all our days together,
Stormy days, perhaps, of courage, with our faces to the weather,
Never any days, but happy, so I thought, if passed with her.
Then the smoke came blowing thickly till it made the wood a
blur.

Still, I did not think of evil, for one could not, living there.
But I said, "The rooks are startled," for their crying filled the
air,

And I wondered, in the meadow, why the cows were not at grass,
Only smoke, down-blowing, bitter, that the birds were loath to
pass.

So I quickened through the meadow to the close that hid the
home
And the smoke drove down in volleys, lifted up, and wreathed
and clomb,
And I could not see, because of it, and what one cannot see
Holds the fear that lives in darkness, so that fear began in me.

And the place was like a death-house save for cawings overhead,
All the cocks and hens were silent and the dogs were like the
dead,
Nothing but the smoke seemed living, thick, and hiding whence
it came,
Bitter with the change of burning, hot upon the cheek from
flame.

Then my fear became a terror and I knew that ill had fallen
From the fate that comes unthought of when the unheard word
is callen,
So I flung the little gate astray and burst the bushes through
Little red-white blossoms flecked me and my face was dashed
with dew.

Then I saw what ill had fallen, for the house had burned to
death,
Though it gleamed with running fire when a falling gave a
breath,
All the roof was sky, the lead dripped, all the empty windows
wide
Spouted smoke, and all was silent, save the volleying rooks that
cried.

This I saw.   I rocked with anguish at the flicking heap that
    glowed.
She was dead among the ashes that the lead drops did corrode.
She was dead, that gave a meaning to the beauty of the spring,
Yet the daffodils still nodded and the blackbirds still did sing.

When the stunning passed, I stumbled to the house's westward
    side
Thinking there to find some neighbour that could tell me how
    she died;
Fearing, too, lest Death the devil who had dealt such murder
    there
Should be hiding there behind me for to clutch me unaware.

There was no one there alive, but my leaping heart was stilled
By the sight of bodies lying in the grass where they were killed.
Drooped into the grass they lay there, pressing close into the
    ground
As the dead do, in the grasses; all my world went spinning round.

Then I saw, that with the bodies, all the ground was heaped and
    strown
With the litter of a house that had been gutted to the bone;
Split and hingeless coffers yawning, linen drooped like people
    dead,
Trinkets broken for their jewels, barrels staved, and crusts
    of bread.

Then a mess of feathers blowing, then the cattle's heads, and
    then
Stunned at all this wreck I hurried to the bodies of the men.
Five were workers of the household, lying dead in her defence;
Roused from sleep, perhaps, in darkness so that death might
    dash them thence.

But the other three were strangers, swarthy, bearded, hook-
nosed, lean,
Wearing white (for night surprisal) over seamen's coats of green;
Moorish-coloured men, still greedy for the prize they died to
snatch;
Clutching broken knives, or grass-blades, or some tatters of
their catch.

Then I moaned aloud, for then I knew the truth, that these
Were the Moorish pirate raiders who had come there from the
seas,
Come upon my love defenceless, by surprise, and I not there.
Come to burn or kill her beauty or to drag her to their lair.

"Dragged away to be a slave," I thought. I saw what she had
seen,
All the good friends lying slaughtered in the young grass dewy
green;
All the cattle killed for provant and the gutted homestead
burning,
And the skinny Moors to drag her to the death of no returning.

Minutes passed, yet still I stood there, when I heard one call my
name,
Amys, once my darling's woman, from her hiding-corner came,
"O," she cried, "They came upon us when the light was growing
gray
And they sacked and burned and slaughtered, and they've
carried her away.

"I was sleeping in the cottage when I heard the noise of men,
And the shots; and I could see them, for the house was blazing
then.
They were like to devils, killing, so I hid, and then I heard
Rollo moaning in the bushes with a face as white as curd.

"He was dying from a bullet, but he said 'Saffee.   Saffee
Pirates, Amys; they were burning and they shot and murdered
    me.
Amys, look where I was murdered, look, they blew away my
    side,
And they burnt the cows in stable.'   Then he moaned until he
    died.

"It was terrible to hear them kill the beasts and pack their prey.
Then they shouldered up their plunder and they sang and
    marched away;
And they took my lady with them as a slave-girl to be sold.
I saw them kill Paloma, they said that she was old.

"Then they went on board their cruiser and she sailed away at
    once.
Look there, beyond the beaches, you see her where she
    runs—"
          *   *   *   *   *   *   *
I saw a peaked sail pointing and feathering oars that flasht
In the blueness of the water that was whitened where they
    gasht.
          *   *   *   *   *   *   *
There they carried my beloved in a pirate ship at sea
To be sold like meat for killing in the markets of Saffee.
Some fire-shrivelled oak-leaves blew lightly past my face,
A beam fell in ruins, the fire roared a space.

I walked down to the water, my heart was torn in two
For the anguish of her future and the nothing I could do.
The ship had leaned a little as she snouted to the spray;
The feathering oars flashed steadily at taking her away.

I took a fisher's boat there was and dragged her down the sand,
I set her sail and took an oar and thrust her from the land,

I headed for the pirate, and the brown weed waved beneath
And the boat trod down the bubbles of the bone between her
  teeth.

I brought them down the land-wind so from the first I gained;
I set a tiny topsail that bowed her till she strained.
My mind was with my darling aboard that ship of fear
In cabin close with curtains where Moormen watched my dear.

Now when they saw me coming they wondered what it meant,
This young man in a fish-boat who followed where they went.
They judged that I was coming to buy the woman free;
So suddenly the oars stopped, they waited on the sea.

I dropped my sail close to them and ranged to easy hail,
Her plunges shivered wrinklings along her spilling sail,
The water running by her had made her shine like gold,
The oar blades poised in order kissed water when she rolled.

A hundred naked rowers stared down their oars at me
With all the bitter hatred the slave has for the free.
The boatswain walked above them, he mocked me, so did they:
The sun had burnt their bodies and yet their look was gray.

So there we rocked together, while she, at every roll,
Moaned from her guns with creakings that shook her to the
  soul;
I did not see my darling; she lay in ward below
Down in the green hung cabin she first joined hands with woe.

The galley plowtered, troubling; the mockings of the slaves
Passed from bench to bench, like bird's cries, her bow-beak
  slapt the waves,

Then her captain came on deck, quick and hard, with snapping
    force,
And a kind of cringe of terror stiffened down those banks of
    oars.

The captain walked the deck; he eyed me for a moment,
He called some Turkish words with a muttered added comment,
Then he called, "Well.   What d'ye want?" in the lingua of the
    sea.
The boatswain leaned and spoke, then they sneered and looked
    at me.

So I stood upon the thwart, and I called, "I want to come
To be comrade to the woman whom you've dragged away from
    home.
Since I cannot set her free, I want only to be near her."
"Ah," he said, "Men buy love dear, but by God you buy it
    dearer.

"Well; you shall;" he spoke in Moorish and a seaman tossed a
    cord,
So I hove myself alongside, scrambled up and climbed aboard.
All were silent, but they watched me; all those eyes above the
    oars
Stared, and all their bitter tushes gnashed beneath them like
    a boar's!

At an order, all the oars clanked aft, and checked, and sliced the
    sea,
The rowers' lips twitched upward, the sheets tugged to be free,
The wrinklings in the sail ran up as it rounded to a breast,
The ship bowed to a billow and snouted through the crest.

My boat was tossed behind us, she bowed and swung away.
The captain stood and mocked me, "Well, since you would, you
    may.

You shall be near your lady, until we fetch to port."
They chained me to the oar-loom upon the after-thwart.

All day, until the twilight, I swung upon the oar;
Above the dropping taffrail I sometimes saw the shore,
Behind me swung the rowers, again and yet again
A gasp, a clank of rollocks and then a cry of pain.

The boatswain walked above us to lash us if we slackened;
With blood of many beatings the rowers' backs were blackened,
Again and yet again came the lash and then the cry,
Then a mutter for revenge would run round the ship and die.

But twilight with her planet that brings quiet to the tired,
Bringing dusk upon the water brought the gift that I desired
For they brought my well-beloved to the deck to breathe the
    air,
Not a half an oar's length from me, so we spoke together there.

"You," she said; "Yes, I, beloved, to be near you over sea.
I have come to be beside you and to help to set you free.
Keep your courage and be certain that the God who took will
    give.
God will dawn and we shall prosper for the living soul will live."

Then they bade me stop my talking and to use my breath to row.
Darkness came upon the water and they took my love below.
Fire in the oar-stirred water swirled in streaks that raced away;
Toppling up and down the taffrail touched the red sky and the
    gray.

Then the wind began to freshen till the shrouds were twanging
    sharp,
Thrilling an unchanging honing like a madman with a harp,
Thrilling on a rising water that was hissing as it rose
To be foamed asunder by us as we struck it down with blows.

Soon we could not row, but rested with the oar blades triced
    above,
Then my soul went from my body to give comfort to my love,
Though indeed the only comfort that my mind could find to say
Was, that God, who makes to-morrow makes it better than
    to-day.

So I yearned towards my darling while I drooped upon my
    bench.
All the galley's length was shaken when the mainsail gave a
    wrench;
Always when I roused, the taffrail toppled up to touch the stars,
And the roaring seas ran hissing, and the planks whined, and
    the spars.

Day by day I rowed the galley, night by night I saw the Pole
Sinking lower in the northward to the sorrow of my soul,
Yet at night I saw my darling when she came on deck to walk,
And our thoughts passt to each other though they would not let
    us talk.

Till early on a morning before the dawn had come
Some foreign birds came crying with strong wings wagging
    home.
Then on the wind a warmness, a sweetness as of cloves,
Blew faintly in the darkness from spice and orange groves.

Then, as they set us rowing, the sun rose over land
That seemed a mist of forest above a gleam of sand.
White houses glittered on it, the pirates cheered to see.
By noon we reached the haven, we anchored in Saffee.

They cloaked my well-beloved and carried her ashore
She slipped a paper to me while brushing past my oar.
I took it, muttering "Courage"; I read it when I dared:
"They mean me for the Khalif. I have to be prepared."

ENSLAVED

They led her up the jetty, she passed out of my sight.
Then they knocked away our irons and worked us till the night,
Unbending sails, unstepping masts, clean-scraping banks, unshipping oars
Rousing casks and loot and cables from the orlop into stores.

When all the gear was warehoused, they marched us up the street,
All sand it was, where dogs lay, that sprang and snapped our feet,
Then lancers came at gallop, they knocked us to the side,
They struck us with their lance-staves to make them room to ride.

Then, as we cleared the roadway, with clatter, riding hard,
With foam flung from the bit-cups, there came the body-guard,
Then splendid in his scarlet the Khalif's self went by
A grand young bird of rapine with a hawk-look in his eye.

A slave said, "There's the Khalif. He's riding north to-night,
To Marrakesh, the vineyard, his garden of delight.
That means a night of quiet to us poor dogs who row,
The guards will take their pleasure and we shall rest below."

Then, in the dusk, they marched us to the quarries of the slaves
Which were dripping shafts in limestone giving passage into caves.
There they left us with our rations to the night that prisoners know
Longing after what was happy far away and long ago.
*   *   *   *   *   *   *
Now often, as I rowed upon the bench,
In tugging back the oar-loom in the stroke,
A rower opposite whose face was French

POEMS

Had signalled to me, with a cheer or joke,
Grinning askant, and tossing back his hair
To shew his white, keen features debonair.

And now that I was sitting on the stone,
He came to where I sat, and sat beside.
"So," he exclaimed, "you eat you heart alone.
I did, at first; but prison kills the pride.
It kills the heart, and all it has to give
Is, hatred, daunted by the will to live.

"I was a courtier in the French King's court
Three years ago; you would not think it now,
To see me rower in a pirate port
Rusting my chain with sweatings from my brow.
But I was once Duhamel, over sea,
And should be still, if they would ransom me.

"I honour you for coming as you did
To save your lady. It was nobly done.
They took her for the Khalif; she is hid
There in the woman's palace; but, my son,
You will not look upon her face again.
Best face the fact, whatever be the pain.

"No, do not speak, for she is lost forever,
Hidden in that dark palace of the King.
Not all the loving in the world would ever
Bring word to her, or help, or anything.
She will be pasture to the King's desires,
Then sold, or given in barter, when he tires.

"A woman in the Khalif's house is dead
To all the world forever; that is truth:
And you (most gallantly) have put your head

Into the trap. Till you have done with youth,
You will be slave, in prison or at sea.
Sickness or death alone will set you free."

"Surely," I said, "since people have escaped
From worser hells than this, I, too, might try.
Fate, that is given to all men partly shaped,
Is man's, to alter daily till he die.
I mean to try to save her. Things which men
Mean with their might, succeed, as this will then."

I saw him look about him with alarm.
"O, not so loud," he said, "for there are spies."
His look of tension passed, he caught my arm,
"I think none heard," he said, "but oh be wise
Slaves have been ganched upon the hooks for less.
This place has devilries men cannot guess.

"But no man, ever, has escaped from here.
To talk of it is death; your friend and you
Are slaves for life, and after many a year,
(At best) when you are both too old to do
The work of slaves, you may be flung abroad,
To beg for broken victuals in the road."

I saw that what he said was certainty.
I knew it, even then, but answered, "Well.
I will at least be near her till I die,
And Life is change, and no man can foretell.
Even if thirty years hence we may meet
It is worth while, and prison shall be sweet."

He looked at me with pleasure, then he sighed
And said, "Well, you deserve her." Then he stared
Across the quarry, trying to decide

If I were fit to see his spirit bared.
Quick glances of suspicion and distrust
Searched at my face, and then he said, "I must.

"I must not doubt you, lad, so listen now.
I have a plan, myself, for leaving this.
I meant to try to-night; I'll shew you how
To save your lady. And to-night there is
Hope, for the Kaliph sleeps at Marrakesh.
When knots are loosened fish can burst the mesh."

So eagerly I plighted faith to try
That very night to help him. "If we fail"
He said, "It will be Fate, who flings the die
Against which nothing mortal can avail.
But we are desperate men whose throws succeed,
Being one with Fate, or Change from Passionate Need."

So we agreed, that when the cave was still,
We would attempt, and having broken prison,
Would raid the women's palace on the hill,
And save my lady ere the sun was risen,
Then put to sea towards some hiding-place
North, in the shoals, where galleys could not chase.

Even as we made an end, another slave,
(They called him English Gerard) joined us there.
Often, upon the toppling of a wave
I'd seen him rowing and had heard him swear.
Forceful he was, with promise in his eye
Of rough capacity and liberty.

"Still talking of escape, I'll bet a crown,"
He said to me; "But you are young, my friend,
We oldsters know we cannot leave the town,
We shall be here until the bitter end.

Give up the hope, lad, better let it be,
No slave has ever broken from Saffee.

"Inland, there's desert, westward there's the sea,
Northward the Moorish towns, and in the south
Swamps and the forest to eternity.
The young colt jibs at iron in his mouth
But has to take it, and the fact for us
Is, that we're slaves, and have to linger thus."

"Just what I told him," said Duhamel, "Just,
My very words. It's bitter but the truth.
We shall be slaves until we turn to dust
Your lady, too, until she loses youth.
Put hope aside, and make what life you can
Being a slave, for slave you are, young man."

"Perhaps," said Gerard, "you were told what comes
Of trying to escape, for men have tried.
They only added to their martyrdoms,
Two got away at Christmas, but they died.
The one they skinned and stuffed, the other hangs
Still, near the gate, upon the ganches' fangs."

"How were they caught," I asked. "They were betrayed,"
Said Gerard. "How? By whom? I cannot tell.
They trusted someone with the plans they made
And he betrayed them, like a fiend from hell.
How do I know it? Well. They left no trace,
And yet the lancers knew their hiding place.

"They went straight to it, straight, and caught them there
As soon as daylight came, when they had gone.
(As you'll be taken if you don't beware)

They keep great hooks to hang the bodies on
Of those who run away, or try, for none
Succeeds, nor can, so you be warned, my son."

He nodded to me, gripped my arm, and went
Back to his place, the other side the cave.
"That was a spy," Duhamel whispered, "sent
To test your spirit as a new-come slave.
I know the man, and if report speaks true
He helped in that betrayal of the two.

"Now seem to sleep and when the cave is quiet
We two will try; they say God helps the mad.
To be a slave to Moors is bitter diet
That poisons men; two bitter years I've had
But before dawn we two will end it, lad.
Now seem to sleep."
                           I cuddled to the stone;
Yet Gerard's voice seemed calling to my bone.

And opening my eyes, I saw him there
Looking intently at me, and he shook
His head at me, as though to say "Beware",
And frowned a passionate warning in a look.
A wind-flaw, blowing through the window, took
The flame within the lantern, that it shed
Bright light on him. Again he shook his head.

The wind blowing in from the sea made the flame like a plume;
The slaves, huddled close, cursed in whispers, with chattering
        teeth,
The wolves of their spirits came stealthy to snarl in the gloom
Over bones of their pleasures long-perished: the sea moaned
        beneath.

And my heart glowed with joy that that night I might rescue
    my love,
Glowed with joy in Duhamel whose cunning would conquer
    the guards.
The wind blew in fresher; a sentry went shuffling above,
Some gamblers crouched tense, while a lean hand flickered the
    cards.

Then one by one the gamblers left their game
The shadows shaken by the blowing flame
Winked on the wall until the lamp blew out.
Wrapping his ankle irons in a clout
(To save his skin) each branded slave prepared
To take his sleep his only comfort spared.

A kind of clearness blowing from the night
Made sleepers' faces bonelike with its light.
A sleeper moaning, twisted with his shoulder
Close to the limestone as the wind grew colder.
Trickles of water glistened down and splashed
Pools on the limestone into rings that flashed.
Often a stirring sleeper struck the bell
Of chain-links upon stones. Deep breathing fell
Like sighing, out of all that misery
Of vermined men who dreamed of being free.
Heavily on the beaches fell the sea.

Then, as the tide came in, the waters seething
Under the quarries, mingled with the breathing,
Until the prison in the rock y-hewen
Seemed like a ship that trod the water's ruin
Trampling the toppling sea, while water creeping
Splashed from the seams in darkness on men sleeping.
Far in the city all the dogs were howling
At that white bird the moon in heaven owling.

Out in the guardhouse soldiers made a dither
About the wiry titter of a zither
Their long-drawn songs were timed with clapping hands.

The water hissed its life out on the sands.
The wheel of heaven with all her glittering turned
The city window-lights no longer burned.
Then one by one the soldiers left their clatter
The moon arose and walked upon the water
The sleepers turned to screen her from their eyes.
A fishing boat sailed past; the fishers' cries
Rang in the darkness of the bay without.
Her sail flapped as she creaked and stood about,
Then eased, then leaned, then strained and stood away.
Deep silence followed, save where breathers lay.

So, lying there, with all my being tense
Prepared to strike, to take my lady thence,
A prompting bade me, not to trust too far
This man Duhamel as a guiding star.
Some little thing in him had jarred on me
A touch (the flesh being raw) hurts cruelly.
And something in his speech or in his bearing
Made me mistrust his steadiness in daring
Or his endurance, or his faith to us.
Some smile or word made me distrustful thus.
Who knows the hidden things within our being
That prompt our brain to safety without seeing,
Hear the unheard and save us without sense?
What fingers touch our strings when we are tense?

Even at that point, Duhamel crept to me,
And whispered, "Come, by morning we'll be free.
Creep down the passage there towards the entry,
See what the guards do while I time the sentry.

I think that all the guards are sleeping sound
But, there's his foot, one sentry goes his round.
And I must time him till I know his beat."
Loitering upon the rampart came the feet
Of some loose-slippered soldier. I could hear
Him halt, humming a tune, grounding his spear.

I listened, while Duhamel urged me on.
"Hurry," he said, "the night will soon be gone;
Watch from the passage what the guards are doing:
I'll time the sentry. There'll be no pursuing
If we can pass the guards with him away.
Beyond the bend he cannot see the bay."

"No," I replied, "yet even if the guard
Be all asleep, it cannot but be hard
For us to pick the lock of that steel grille
Without their waking. We cannot be still
Crouched in the puddle, scraping at the lock.
The guards will wake and kill us at a knock."

"Hush," said Duhamel, "Let me whisper close.
I did not dare before for fear of those,
(The rowers and the spies), I have a key
That will unlock the grating silently,
Making no noise at all in catch or ward.
Now creep along and spy upon the guard."

"A key?" said I. My first suspicions died.
"Yes," said the man, "I slipped it from his side,
While he was checking us this afternoon.
Courage, my son, she'll be in safety soon."
He shewed a key, and urged me to be gone
Down the gaunt gashway carven in the stone,
A darkness in the else half-glimmering lime,

Where drops, each minute splashing, told the time.
There, in the darkness somewhere, lay the gate
Where courage and the moment might make Fate.

I rose, half-doubting, upon hands and knees;
The blood within my temples sang like bees;
I heard my heart. I saw Duhamel's face,
Dark eyes in focus in a whitish space,
Watching me close. I doubted, even then.
Then with the impulse which transfigures men,
Doubt, hesitation, terror passed. I crawled
Into the dripping tunnel limestone-walled.

A cold drop spattered on my neck; the wet
Struck chilly where my hands and knees were set.
I crawled into a darkness like a vault
Glimmering and sweating like a rock of salt.

I crept most thief-like till the passage turned.
There, in a barrèd greyness, I discerned
The world without, shut from me by the grille.
I stopped, most thief-like, listening.

                      All was still;
The quarry I had left was still as stone.
The melancholy water-drip alone
Broke silence near me, and ahead the night
Was silent in the beauty of its light,
Across which fell the black of prison bars.

I crawled ten paces more and saw the stars
Above the guard-hut in the quarry pit:
The hut was still, it had no lantern lit.
I crawled again with every nerve intent.

The cleanly sea-wind bringing pleasant scent
Blew through the grille with little specks of sand.
Each second I expected the word "Stand."
That, or a shot, but still, no challenge came.
The twilight of the moon's unearthly flame
Burned steadily; the palm-leaves on the hut
Rustled in gusts, the crazy door was shut.
The guards were either sleeping or not there.

I peered out through the grille and drank the air
For any scent that might betray a guard
Hidden in ambush near me keeping ward;
But no scent, save the cleanness of the sea,
Blew on the night wind blowing in on me.
There was no trace of man.

                    I watched and listened
The water dropped, the trickling passage glistened,
The coldness of the iron pressed my brow.
Then, as I listened, (I can hear it now),
A strangled cry such as a dreamer cries
When the dream binds him that he cannot rise,
Gurgled behind me in the sleepers' cave.
A failing hand that struggled with the grave
Beat on the floor, then fluttered, then relaxed,
Limp as an altar ox a priest has axed.
No need to say that someone had been killed
That was no dream.

                   Yet all the cave was stilled.
Nobody spoke, or called, or ran to aid.
The fingers of the palm leaves ticked and played
On the hut-roof, but yet no guard appeared.
I started to crawl back, because I feared.
I knew that someone must have heard that calling

Of the killed blood upon the midnight falling.
"I shall be judged the killer," so I thought.

So crawling swiftly back like one distraught,
I groped that tunnel where the blackness made
Me feel each inch before my hand was laid.
There was no gleam, save wetness on the wall,
No noise but heart beat or the dropping's fall.
Blackness and silence tense with murder done,
Tense with a soul that had not yet begun
To know the world without the help of clay.
I was in terror in that inky way.

Then suddenly, while stretching out my hand
The terror brought my heart's blood to a stand.
I touched a man.
                        His face was turned to me.
He whispered, "To the grille. I have the key."
So, without speech I turned; he followed after.
I trembled at the droppings from the rafter.
Each noise without seemed footsteps in pursuit.
The palm-leaves fluttered like a running foot.
The moonlight held her lantern to betray us.
A stricken stone was as a sword to slay us.
Then at the grille we paused that I could see
That it was not Duhamel there with me
But English Gerard.

                        "Do not speak," he said;
"Don't think about Duhamel; he is dead.
This key, that should unlock, is sticking: try."
With shaking hands I took the clicket, I.
A lean cogged bolt of iron jangled bright
By shaking in the key-ring, day and night;
It stuck in the knobbed latch and would not lift.

All kinds of terror urged me to be swift,
Fear of the guards and of the darkness dying,
And of Duhamel's body mutely crying
The thin red cry of murdered blood and bone
Piping in darkness to make murder known.
But there the clicket jammed the iron socket
Nor could my hand withdraw it or unlock it.
"Let me," said Gerard; then with guile and skill
He coaxed the knobbed iron from the grille
"It does not fit," he muttered; "after all."
Outside, within his roost, a cock did call
His warning to the ghosts, and slept again,
The stars that glittered in the sky like grain
Seemed paler, and the ticking time sped on
To the guard's waking and the darkness gone
With nothing done.

                    Then Gerard turned to me
"Though this is wrong, Duhamel had the key,
And has it still about him as I guess
Tied to his flesh or hidden in his dress.
Wait here, while I go rummage through his clothes."

A sleeper, tossing, jabbered broken oaths
Then slept, while Gerard crawled.
                              I was alone
Afraid no more, but anxious to the bone.

And looking out I saw a sentry come
Slowly towards the grille. I cowered numb
Back into blackness pressed against the wall.
I heard the measure of his footsteps fall
Along the quarry to me. I could see
The tenseness of his eyes turned full on me
I felt that he must see me and give speech.

His hand, that shook the grille, was in my reach.
He peered within to see if all were well.
Wept as though spat a drop of water fell.
He peered into the blackness where I stood,
Then, having tried the lock, he tossed his hood,
Crouched at the grille and struck a light, and lit
Tinder, and blew the glowing end of it
Till all his face was fierce in the strong glow;
He sucked the rank tobacco lighted so,
And stood a moment blowing bitter smoke.
I hardly dared to breathe lest I should choke.
I longed to move, but dared not.   Had I stirred
Even a finger's breadth, he must have heard.
He must have touched me had he thrust his hand
Within the grille to touch the wall he scanned.

Then, slowly, muttering to himself, he took
Three steps away, then turned for one more look
Straight at the grille and me.   I counted ten.
Something within the passage moved him then
Because he leaned and peered as though unsure.
Then, stepping to the grille-work's embrasure,
He thrust his face against the iron grid,
And stared into the blackness where I hid,
And softly breathed, "Duhamel."

                                        As he spoke
A passing cloud put dimness as of smoke
Over the moon's face.   No-one answered him,
A drip-drop spat its wetness in the dim.
He paused to call again, then turned away.
He wandered slowly up the quarry way
But at the bend he stopped to rest his bones.
He sat upon the bank and juggled stones
For long long minutes.   Gerard joined me there

We watched the sentry tossing stones in air
To catch them on his hand's back as they fell.
We wished him in the bottom pit of hell.
At last he rose and sauntered round the bend.
The falling of his footsteps had an end
At last, and Gerard spoke, "I have the key."

The cogs caught in the locket clickily,
The catch fell back, the heavy iron gave.
We pushed the grille and stept out of the grave
Into the moonlight where the wind was blowing.
"Hurry," I whispered, for the cocks were crowing
In unseen roosts, the morning being near.
We climbed the bank.
                         "This way," said Gerard, "here.

Now, down the slope. We dodge the sentry so.
Now through the water where the withies grow.
Now we are out of sight; now we can talk."
We changed our crouching running to a walk.

He led me up a slope where rats carousing
Squealed or showed teeth among the tumbled housing,
Half ruined wooden huts, or lime-washed clay.
We turned from this into a trodden way
Pale in the moonlight, where the dogs that prowled
Snarled as we passed, then eyed the moon and howled.
Below us, to our right, the harbour gleamed,
In front, pale with the moon, the city dreamed,
Roof upon roof, with pointing fingers white,
The minarets, frost-fretted with the light,
With many a bubbled dome-top like a shell
Covering the hillside to the citadel.

"There, to the left," said Gerard, "where the trees are,
That whiteness is the palace of the Cæsar,

His gardens and his fishpools. That long building
Flanked by the domes that glitter so with gilding
Is where the women are.   She will be there.
But courage, comrade, never yield to care,
We'll set her free, before the morning breaks,
But oh, my son, no more of your mistakes.
What made you trust Duhamel as you did?
Well, he is dead.   The world is better rid
Of men like him.   He tempted and betrayed
Those two poor souls last year.

                       Ah, when he bade
You go to watch the guard I studied him.
He was a bitter viper, supple—slim.
When he had judged that you had reached the entry,
He stole towards the grate and called the sentry,
'Hussein, Hussein—' but Hussein never heard.
He called him twice, but never called the third
I stopped his calling, luckily for you."
"Yes, but" (I said), "what did he mean to do,
Calling the sentry? What could that have done?"
"Caught you in trying to escape, my son,
The thing they love to do from time to time.
They reckon that examples stop the crime.
One caught and skinned makes many fear to try.
They would have flayed your skin off cruelly
In face of all these slaves, to daunt them down.
Then you'd have hung a dying in the town
Nailed to some post, two days, perhaps, or three,
With thirst and flies.

                    But let Duhamel be,
Bad though he was, misfortune tempts a soul
Worse than we think, and few men can control
Their virtue, being slave; and he had been
A Knight of France, a courtier of the Queen.

He must have suffered to have fallen so,
A slave, a spy on slaves; we cannot know
Thank God, what power of sinking lies in us.
God keep us all."

    So talking to me thus,
He turned me leftward from the citadel
Uphill. He said, "I know this city well,
There is the Khalif's palace straight ahead.
How many days I've staggered nearly dead
From thirst, and from the sun, and from the load,
Up to the palace-gates along this road,
Bearing the plunder of the cruise to store,
After a month of tugging at the oar,
But now, please God, I shall not come again."

Our talking stopped; we turned into a lane.
High, white-washed walls rose up on either side,
The narrow gash between was four feet wide,
And there at sprawl within the narrow way
With head in hood a sleeping beggar lay.
We stepped across his body heedfully
Deep in his dream he muttered drowsily.

We tip-toed on. The wall-tops, high above,
White in the quiet moonlight, hid my love.
We crept like worms in darkness yard by yard,
Still as the dead, but that our hearts beat hard.
And, spite of self, my teeth clickt from the flood
Of quick excitement running in my blood.
We were so near her, and the peril came
Close, with the moment that would prove the same.

The lane turned sharply twice. In shadow dark,
With shiverings of singing like a lark,

A fountain sprang, relented, sprinkled, bubbled,
In some cool garden that the moonlight troubled,
Unseen by us, although a smell of roses
Warm on the wind, stole to us from its closes.
Then came a wood-smoke smell, and mixed therewith
Gums from the heart's blood of the sinnam's pith.
And Gerard touched me. We had reached the place.
The woman's palace-wall was there in face
The garden-wall merged with it, moonlight-topped,
Just where the two together merged we stopped.
Then, as we stood there, breathing, we could hear,
Beyond the wall, some footsteps loitering near,
Some garden sentry slowly paced his watch
Crooning a love song; I could smell the match
That smouldered in the linstock at his hand.

His footsteps passed away upon the sand
Slowly, with pauses, for he stopped to eat
The green buds of the staric on his beat.
When he had gone, a cock crowed in the lane.
"It will be morning when he crows again."
Was in our thoughts: we had full little time.

Some joist-holes gave us foothold, we could climb
Without much trouble to the wall's flat top,
There we lay still, to let the plaster drop,
And see what dangers lay below us there.

The garden of the palace breathed sweet air
Under our perch, the fountain's leaping glitter
Shone; a bird started with a frightened twitter.
Alleys of blossomed fruit trees girt a cool
White marble screen about a bathing pool,
The palace rose beyond among its trees,
Splay-fronded figs and dates and cypresses.

Close to our left hands was the Woman's House.
We crept along our wall-top perilous
Till we could touch the roof that hid my love
A teaken joist-end jutted out above.
We swung ourselves upon the roof thereby.
The dewy wet flat house-top faced the sky.
We crouched together there.

Sweet smoke was wreathing
Out of a trap-door near us; heavy breathing
Came from a woman sleeping near the trap.
I crept to her, not knowing what might hap.
She was an old Moor woman with primmed lips,
And foul white hair, and hennaed finger tips
That clutched a dark hair blanket to her chin.

I crept to the trap-door and peered within.
A ladder led within.   A lantern burning
Shewed us a passage leading to a turning
But open to the garden at one end.

Even as we peered, a man came round the bend,
Walked slowly down that lamp-lit corridor,
And stood to watch the garden at the door.
We saw his back within that moonlit square.
He had a curving sword which glittered bare.
He stood three minutes still, watching the night,
Each beating second made the east more light.
He cracked and relished nuts or melon seeds.

The hoof-sparks of the morning's running steeds
Made a pale dust now in the distant east
But still the man stood cracking at his feast
Nut after nut; Then flinging broken shell
Into the rose-walk, clicking as it fell,
He turned towards us up the passage dim.

There at the trap we crouched right over him,
And as he passed beneath, his fingers tried
A door below us in the passage-side.
Then, slowly loitering on, he reached and passed
The passage turning; he was gone at last
His footsteps died away; they struck on stone
In some far cloister; we were left alone.

Then, while our leaping hearts beat like to drums
We took the gambler's way, that takes what comes.
We slid into the trap and down the stair,
Steep, like a loft's; eleven rungs there were.
We stood within the passage at the door
Tried by the guard that little while before.

Within, there was a rustling and a chinking,
(Like the glass dangles that the wind sets clinking)
And something tense there was within; the throbbing
Of hearts in a despair too deep for sobbing
We felt it there before we pressed the latch.

The teaken bar rose stiffly from its catch.
We slipt within and closed the door again.
We were within the dwelling place of pain,
Among the women whom the Moors had taken,
The broken-hearts, despairing and forsaken.
The desolate that cried where no man heard.

Nobody challenged, but some women stirred.
It was so dark at first, after the moon.
A smoking censer, swinging, creaked a croon,
There was a hanging lamp of beaten brass
That gave dim light through scraps of coloured glass
I saw a long low room with many a heap
Dark, on the floor, where women lay asleep

On silken cushions. Round the wall there ran
(Dark, too, with cushioned women) a divan,
And women stirred and little chains were shaken.

What horror 'tis, to prisoners, to waken
Out of the dreams of home back to the chain,
Back to the iron and the mill again,
In some far land among one's enemies.
I knew that then; those women made me wise.

We stared into the twilight till our eyes
Could see more clearly: no one challenged us.
But standing back against the doorway thus,
I saw the warden of the room, asleep,
Close to me, on the cushions, breathing deep,
Her hard face made like iron by the gloom.
An old grim Moor that warden of the room,
A human iron fettered on the poor.
Far down the room a fetter touched the floor.

Even in the gloom I knew that she was there,
My April of a woman with bright hair;
She sat upright against the wall alone
By burning meditation turned to stone,
Staring ahead and when I touched her shoulder
Her body (stiffened like a corpse and colder)
Seemed not herself, her mind seemed far away.

There was no need to talk, but to essay
The light steel chain that linked her to the wall.
We gripped it, heaving, till its links were gall
Biting across our hands, but still we drave
She, I and Gerard heaving till it gave
The leaded staple snapped across the shank.

The loosed chain struck the flooring with a clank.
We all lay still, my arm about my own.
"Who's moving there? Be silent," snapped the crone.

Cross with the slave who had awakened her
She stared towards us. We could hear her stir,
Craning towards us, but she could not see
More than the cushions tumbled there with me.
She thought, perhaps, "That fair one shook her chain."
She growled, "I'll beat you, if you stir again.
A Moorish whip upon your Christian skin."

I saw her clutch her blanket to her chin
Turn to her side and settle to her rest.
The dawn, that brings the skylark from her nest
Was flying with bright feet that ever hasted.
Each moment there meant happy chances wasted,
Yet still we had to stay until she slept.

When she had fallen to a doze we crept
Stealthily to the door on hands and knees.
All of those women came from over seas.
We could not waken them to share our chance.
Not Peru's silver nor the fields of France
Could buy a place in our society.
One tender feeling might have made us die
All three, and been no kindness to the fourth:
Compassions perish when the wind is north.

Close to the door, a woman leaned and caught
My darling's hand and kissed it swift as thought
And whispered, "O, good luck," and then was still.
She had no luck, but O she had good will.
We blest her in our hearts.

     The warder stirred
Growling but dozing lightly, then we heard
Outside the door, within three feet of us,
The footsteps of the sentry perilous,
The clinking of his scabbard lightly touching
Some metal button, then his fingers clutching
The teaken catch to try if it were home.

We stood stone-still expecting him to come.
He did not come, he pushed the door and passed,
Treading this beat exactly like the last,
To loiter at the door to crack and spit.

The time dragged by till he had done with it.
Then back he came, and once again he shook
The catch upon its socket, then he took
His way along the passage out of hearing.

The room 'gan glimmer from the dawning nearing
The warder struggled with a dream and cried
The lamp-flame purred from want of oil and died.
And she, the woman who had kissed her hand,
Whispered, "O go, for God's sake, do not stand
One moment more, but go.　God help you free."

We crept out of the prison silently,
Gerard the last, who closed the door behind us,
The crowing of a cock came to remind us
That it was morning now with daylight breaking
The leaves all shivering and birds awaking.
We climbed the ladder.

     Its eleven rungs
Called to the Moors of us with all their tongues.
"Wake," "Wake;" "They fly."　"The three of them are
 flying."

"O broken house," "O sleepers, thieves are trying
To take the Khalif's treasure." "Guards," "Awake."
"They rob the women." "For the prophet's sake."
"Slaughter these Christians." Thus the ladder spoke
Three times aloud yet nobody awoke
Even the hag upon the roof was still.

Now the red cock of dawning triumphed shrill
And little ends of landwind shook the leaves.
White through the cypress gleamed the palace eaves.
The dim and dewy beauty of the blossom,
Shy with the daybreak, trembled in its bosom,
Some snowy petals loitered to the ground.
The city houses had a wakening sound
Some smoke was rising, and we heard the stirs
Made at the gates by country marketers;
Only a moment's twilight yet remained.

The supple links that held my darling chained
Served as a rope to help her down the wall.
Our hearts stood still to hear the plaster fall
But down we scrambled safely to the lane.
We heard the hag upon the roof complain
She called strange names and listened for reply.
We heard her tread the ladder heavily
It was her rising time, perhaps, we thought.

And now the dangers that the daylight brought
Came thick upon us; for our foreign dress
Betrayed us at each step beyond a guess,
Even to be seen was certain death to us.
We hid my darling's face, and hasting thus
Kept up the narrow lane as Gerard bade.
He said, "Beyond, the city wall is laid
Heaped in the ditch and we can cross it there.

It fell from rottenness and dis-repair.
They set no guard there—or they did not set.
They will not notice us, and we can get
Out to the tombs and hide inside a vault."

In overbrimming beauty without fault
The sun brought colour to that dingy hive.
It made the black tree green, the sea alive,
The huts like palaces, but us who fled
Like ghosts at cockcrow hasting to the dead.

The lane had ceased. We reached an open space,
The greenish slope, the horses' baiting place,
Between the city and the palace wall.
The hill dipped sharply in a steepish fall
Down to the houses, and the grass was worn
With hoofs, and littered with the husks of corn.
"Now, slowly," Gerard said, "for Moors go slowly."

There trembling in its blueness dim and holy
Lay the great water bursting on the Mole
Her tremblings came as thoughts come in a soul.
There was our peace, there was the road to home,
That never trodden trembling bright with foam.
"There lies the road," said Gerard, "now, come on."

The high leaves in the trees above us shone,
For now the sun had climbed the eastern hill,
The coldness of the dawn was with us still.
We walked along the grass towards an alley
Between high walls beyond a tiny valley.

Fronting this alley's mouth our sloping grass
Dipped down and up, a little gut there was
Down which we slithered and from which we climbed.

And just as we emerged, exactly timed,
Just as we drew my darling to the top,
There came a noise that made our pulses stop.

For down towards us, blocking all the road,
Their horses striking sparks out as they strode,
Came lancers clattering with their hands held high,
Their knees bent up, and many a sharp quick cry;
The pennons in their lance heads flapped like flame.

Three ranks in twos and then a swordsman came,
Then one who held a scarlet banner; then
One in a scarlet cloak, a King of men.

It was the Khalif's self, returning home,
His rein had smeared his stallion's crest with foam,
I noticed that.   He was not twenty yards
From us.   He saw us

                    At a sign his guards
Rode round us; bade us stand; there was no hope.

"Our luck," said Gerard.   Then they took a rope
And hitched our wrists together.   Then they led
The three of us down-hearted like the dead
Before the Khalif's self.   The swordsman bared
His right arm to the shoulder and prepared.

The Khalif stared at us, and we at him
We were defiant at him, he was grim.
A hawk-like fellow, like a bird of prey,
A hawk to strike, a swift to get away.
His clean brown face (with blood beneath the brown),
Puckered, his thin lips tightened in a frown,
He knew without our telling, what we were.

The swordsman looked for word to kill us there.

I saw the lancers' glances at their chief.
Death on the instant would have seemed relief
To that not knowing what her fate would be
After the sword had made an end of me.

The Khalif's face grew grimmer; then he said
"Bring them with us." The swordsman sheathed his blade.

They took us to the palace, to a chamber
Smelling of bruisèd spice and burning amber,
There slaves were sent to fetch the newly risen
Servants and warders of the woman's prison.
The white of death was on them when they came.

The Khalif lightened on them with quick flame.
Harsh though she was, I sorrowed for the crone,
For she was old, a woman, and alone,
And came, in age, upon disgrace through me;
I know not what disgrace, I did not see
Those crones again, I doubt not they were whipt
For letting us escape them while they slept.
Perhaps they killed the sentry. Who can tell?
The devil ever keeps the laws in hell.
They dragged them out to justice one by one.
However bitter was the justice done
I doubt not they were thankful to be quit
(At cost of some few pangs) the fear of it.
Then our turn came.

           The Khalif's fury raged
Because our eyes had seen those women caged,
Because our Christian presence had defiled
The Woman's House and somehow had beguiled

A woman-slave, his victim, out of it,
Against all Moorish law and Holy Writ
If we had killed his son it had been less.

He rose up in his place and rent his dress
"Let them be ganched upon the hooks," he cried,
"Throughout to-day, but not till they have died.
Then gather all the slaves, and flay these three
Alive, before them, that the slaves may see
What comes to dogs who try to get away.
So, ganch the three."

        Then Gerard answered, "Stay.
Before you fling us to the hooks, hear this.
There are two laws, and men may go amiss
Either by breaking or by keeping one.
There is man's law by which man's work is done.
Your galleys rowed, your palace kept in state
Your victims ganched or headed on the gate
And accident has bent us to its yoke.
"We break it: death: but it is better broke.

"You know, you Khalif, by what death you reign,
What force of fraud, what cruelty of pain,
What spies and prostitutes support your power,
And help your law to run its little hour,
We, who are but ourselves, defy it all.

"We were free people till you made us thrall
I was a sailor whom you took at sea
While sailing home. This woman that you see
You broke upon with murder in the night
To drag her here to die for your delight,
This young man is her lover.
        When he knew
That she was taken by your pirate crew

He followed her to save her, or at least
Be near her in her grief. Man is a beast
And women are his pasture by your law.
This young man was in safety, but he saw
His darling taken to the slave-girls' pen
Of weeping in the night and beasts of men.
He gave up everything, risked everything,
Came to your galley, took the iron ring,
Rowed at the bitter oar-loom as a slave,
Only for love of her, for hope to save
Her from one bruise of all the many bruises
That fall upon a woman when she loses
Those whom your gang of bloodhounds made her lose.

"Knowing another law we could not choose
But stamp your law beneath our feet as dust,
Its bloodshed and its rapine and its lust,
For one clean hour of struggle to be free;
She for her passionate pride of chastity,
He for his love of her, and I because
I'm not too old to glory in the cause
Of generous souls who have harsh measure meted.

"We did the generous thing and are defeated.
Boast, then, to-night when you have drunken deep,
Between the singing woman's song and sleep,
That you have tortured to the death three slaves
Who spat upon your law and found their graves
Helping each other in the generous thing.
No mighty triumph for a boast, O King."

Then he was silent while the Khalif stared.
Never before had any being dared
To speak thus to him. All the courtiers paled.
We, who had died, expected to be haled

To torture there and then before the crowd.
It was so silent that the wind seemed loud
Clicking a lose slat in the open shutter.
I heard the distant breakers at their mutter
Upon the Mole, I saw my darling's face
Steady and proud; a breathing filled the place,
Men drawing breath until the Khalif spoke.
His torn dress hung upon him like a cloak
He spoke at last. "You speak of law," he said.
"By climates and by soils the laws are made.
Ours is a hawk-law suited to the land,
This rock of hawks or eyrie among sand,
I am a hawk, the hawk law pleases me.

"But I am man, and, being man, can be
Moved, sometimes, Christian, by the law which makes
Men who are suffering from man's mistakes,
Brothers sometimes.
                         I had not heard this tale
Of you, the lover, following to jail
The woman whom you loved. You bowed your neck
Into the iron fettered to the deck,
And followed her to prison, all for love?

"Allah, who gives men courage from above,
Has surely blessed you, boy.

                         "And you, his queen;
Without your love his courage had not been.
Your beauty and your truth prevailed on him.
Allah has blessed you, too.

                         "And you, the grim
Killer of men at midnight, you who speak
To Kings as peers with colour in your cheek,

ENSLAVED

Allah made you a man who helps his friends.
"God made you all. I will not thwart his ends
You shall be free.

               Hear all. These folk are free.
You Emir, fit a xebec for the sea
To let them sail at noon.

                  Go where you will.
And lest my rovers should molest you still,
Here is my seal that they shall let you pass."

Throughout the room a sudden murmur was
A gasp of indrawn breath and shifting feet.
So life was given back, the thing so sweet
The undrunk cup that we were longing for.

My darling spoke, "O Khalif, one gift more.
After this bounty that our hearts shall praise
At all our praying-times by nights and days
I ask yet more, O raiser from the dead.
There in your woman's prison as we fled
A hopeless woman blessed us. It is said
That blessings from the broken truly bless.
Khalif, we would not leave in hopelessness
One whose great heart could bless us even then
Even as we left her in the prison pen.
She wished us fortune from a broken heart.
Let her come with us, Khalif, when we start."
"Go, you," the Khalif said, "and choose her forth."

At noon the wind was blowing to the north,
A swift felucca with a scarlet sail
Was ready for us, deep with many a bale,
Of gold and spice and silk, the great King's gifts.
The banners of the King were on her lifts.
The King and all his court rode down to see
Us four glad souls put seawards from Saffee.

In the last glowing of the sunset's gold
We looked our last upon that pirate hold;
The palace gilding shone awhile like fire,
We were at sea with all our heart's desire
Beauty and friendship and the dream fulfilled.
The golden answer to the deeply willed.
The purely longed for, hardly tried for thing.
Into the dark our sea boat dipped her wing
Polaris climbed out of the dark and shone,
Then came the moon, and now Saffee was gone
With all hell's darkness hidden by the sea.

O beautiful is love and to be free
Is beautiful, and beautiful are friends.
Love, freedom, comrades, surely make amends
For all these thorns through which we walk to death.
God let us breathe your beauty with our breath.

All early in the Maytime when daylight comes at four,
We blessed the hawthorn blossom that welcomed us ashore,
O beautiful in this living that passes like the foam
It is to go with sorrow yet come with beauty home.

THE HOUNDS OF HELL

ABOUT the crowing of the cock,
  When the shepherds feel the cold,
A horse's hoofs went clip-a-clock
  Along the Hangman's wold.

The horse-hoofs trotted on the stone,
  The hoof-sparks glittered by,
And then a hunting horn was blown
  And hounds broke into cry.

There was a strangeness in the horn,
  A wildness in the cry,
A power of devilry forlorn
  Exulting bloodily.

A power of night that ran a prey
  Along the Hangman's hill.
The shepherds heard the spent buck bray
  And the horn blow for the kill.

They heard the worrying of the hounds
  About the dead beast's bones;
Then came the horn, and then the sounds
  Of horse-hoofs treading stones.

"What hounds are these, that hunt the night?"
  The shepherds asked in fear:
"Look, there are calkins clinking bright;
  They must be coming here."

The calkins clinkered to a spark,
   The hunter called the pack;
The sheep-dogs' fells all bristled stark
   And all their lips went back.

"Lord God," the shepherds said, "They come;
   And see what hounds he has;
All dripping bluish fire, and dumb,
   And nosing to the grass.

"And trotting scatheless through the gorse,
   And bristling in the fell:
Lord, it is death upon the horse,
   And they're the hounds of hell!"

They shook to watch them as they sped,
   All black against the sky;
A horseman with a hooded head
   And great hounds padding by.

When daylight drove away the dark
   And larks went up and thrilled,
The shepherds climbed the wold to mark
   What beast the hounds had killed.

They came to where the hounds had fed,
   And in that trampled place
They found a pedlar lying dead
   With horror in his face.

There was a farmer on the wold
   Where all the brooks begin,
He had a thousand sheep from fold
   Out grazing on the whin.

The next night, as he lay in bed
   He heard a canterer come
Trampling the wold-top with a tread
   That sounded like a drum.

He thought it was a post that rode,
   So turned him to his sleep,
But the canterer in his dreams abode
   Like horse-hoofs running sheep.

And in his dreams a horn was blown
   And feathering hounds replied,
And all his wethers stood like stone
   In rank on the hillside.

Then, while he struggled still with dreams,
   He saw his wethers run
Before a pack cheered on with screams,
   The thousand sheep as one.

So, leaping from his bed in fear,
   He flung the window back,
And he heard a death-horn blowing clear
   And the crying of a pack.

And the thundering of a thousand sheep,
   All mad and running wild
To the stone-pit seven fathoms deep,
   Whence all the town is tiled.

After them came the hounds of hell
   With hell's own fury filled;
Into the pit the wethers fell
   And all but three were killed.

The hunter blew his horn a note
    And laughed against the moon;
The farmer's breath caught in his throat,
    He fell into a swoon.

The next night when the watch was set
    A heavy rain came down,
The leaden gutters dripped with wet
    Into the shuttered town.

So close the shutters were, the chink
    Of lamplight scarcely showed;
The men at fireside heard no clink
    Of horse-hoofs on the road.

They heard the creaking hinge complain
    And the mouse that gnawed the floor,
And the limping footsteps of the rain
    On the stone outside the door.

And on the wold the rain came down
    Till trickles streakt the grass:
A traveller riding to the town
    Drew rein to let it pass.

The wind sighed in the fir-tree tops,
    The trickles sobb'd in the grass,
The branches ran with showers of drops;
    No other noise there was.

Till up the wold the traveller heard
    A horn blow faint and thin;
He thought it was the curlew bird
    Lamenting to the whin;

And when the far horn blew again,
  He thought an owl hallooed,
Or a rabbit gave a shriek of pain
  As the stoat leapt in the wood.

But when the horn blew next, it blew
  A trump that split the air,
And hounds gave cry to an Halloo—
  The hunt of hell was there.

"Black," (said the traveller), "black and swift,
  Those running devils came;
Scoring to cry with hackles stifft,
  And grin-jowls dripping flame."

They settled to the sightless scent,
  And up the hill a cry
Told where the frightened quarry went,
  Well knowing it would die.

Then presently a cry rang out,
  And a mort blew for the kill;
A shepherd with his throat torn out
  Lay dead upon the hill.

When this was known, the shepherds drove
  Their flocks into the town;
No man, for money or for love,
  Would watch them on the down.

But night by night the terror ran,
  The townsmen heard them still;
Nightly the hell-hounds hunted man
  And the hunter whooped the kill.

The men who lived upon the moor
   Would waken to the scratch
Of hounds' claws digging at the door.
   Or scraping at the latch.

And presently no man would go
   Without doors after dark,
Lest hell's black hunting horn should blow,
   And hell's black bloodhounds mark.

They shivered round the fire at home,
   While out upon the bent
The hounds with black jowls dropping foam
   Went nosing to the scent.

Men let the hay crop run to seed,
   And the corn crop sprout in ear,
And the root crop choke itself in weed
   That hell-hound hunting year.

Empty to heaven lay the wold,
   Village and church grew green,
The courtyard flagstones spread with mould,
   And weeds sprang up between.

And sometimes when the cock had crowed,
   And the hillside stood out grey,
Men saw them slinking up the road,
   All sullen from their prey.

A hooded horseman on a black,
   With nine black hounds at heel,
After the hell-hunt going back
   All bloody from their meal.

And in men's minds a fear began
   That hell had over-hurled
The guardians of the soul of man
   And come to rule the world.

With bitterness of heart by day,
   And terror in the night,
And the blindness of a barren way
   And withering of delight.

St. Withiel lived upon the moor,
   Where the peat-men live in holes;
He worked among the peat-men poor,
   Who only have their souls.

He brought them nothing but his love
   And the will to do them good,
But power filled him from above,
   His very touch was food.

Men told St. Withiel of the hounds
   And how they killed their prey.
He thought them far beyond his bounds,
   So many miles away.

Then one whose son the hounds had killed
   Told him the tale at length;
St. Withiel pondered why God willed
   That hell should have such strength.

Then one, a passing traveller, told
   How, since the hounds had come,
The church was empty on the wold,
   And all the priests were dumb.

St. Withiel rose at this, and said,
    "This priest will not be dumb;
My spirit will not be afraid
    Though all hell's devils come."

He took his stick and out he went,
    The long way to the wold,
Where the sheep-bells clink upon the bent
    And every wind is cold.

He past the rivers running red
    And the mountains standing bare;
At last the wold-land lay ahead,
    Un-yellowed by the share.

All in the brown October time
    He clambered to the weald;
The plum lay purpled into slime,
    The harvest lay in field.

Trampled by many-footed rain,
    The sun-burnt corn lay dead;
The myriad finches in the grain
    Rose bothering at his tread.

The myriad finches took a sheer
    And settled back to food:
A man was not a thing to fear
    In such a solitude.

The hurrying of their wings died out,
    A silence took the hill;
There was no dog, no bell, no shout,
    The windmill's sails were still.

The gate swung creaking on its hasp,
  The pear splashed from the tree,
In the rotting apple's heart the wasp
  Was drunken drowsily.

The grass upon the cart-wheel ruts
  Had made the trackways dim,
The rabbits ate and hopped their scuts,
  They had no fear of him.

The sunset reddened in the west;
  The distant depth of blue
Stretched out and dimmed; to twiggy nest
  The rooks in clamour drew.

The oakwood in his mail of brass
  Bowed his great crest and stood;
The pine-tree saw St. Withiel pass,
  His great bole blushed like blood.

Then tree and wood alike were dim,
  Yet still St. Withiel strode;
The only noise to comfort him
  Were his footsteps on the road.

The crimson in the west was smoked,
  The west-wind heaped the wrack,
Each tree seemed like a murderer cloaked
  To stab him in the back.

Darkness and desolation came
  To dog his footsteps there;
The dead leaves rustling called his name,
  The death-moth brushed his hair.

The murmurings of the wind fell still;
　　He stood and stared around:
He was alone upon the hill,
　　On devil-haunted ground.

What was the whitish thing which stood
　　In front, with one arm raised,
Like death a-grinning in a hood?
　　The saint stood still and gazed.

"What are you?" said St. Withiel, "Speak!"
　　Not any answer came
But the night-wind making darkness bleak,
　　And the leaves that called his name.

A glow shone on the whitish thing,
　　It neither stirred nor spoke:
In spite of faith, a shuddering
　　Made the good saint to choke.

He struck the whiteness with his staff—
　　It was a withered tree:
An owl flew from it with a laugh,
　　The darkness shook with glee.

The darkness came all round him close
　　And cackled in his ear:
The midnight, full of life none knows,
　　Was very full of fear.

The darkness cackled in his heart,
　　That things of hell were there,
That the startled rabbit played a part
　　And the stoat's leap did prepare—

Prepare the stage of night for blood
  And the mind of night for death,
For a spirit trembling in the mud,
  In an agony for breath.

A terror came upon the saint,
  It stripped his spirit bare;
He was sick body standing faint,
  Cold sweat and stiffened hair.

He took his terror by the throat
  And stamped it underfoot;
Then, far away, the death-horn's note
  Quailed like a screech-owl's hoot.

Still far away that devil's horn
  Its quavering death-note blew,
But the saint could hear the crackling thorn
  That the hounds trod as they drew.

"Lord, it is true," St. Withiel moaned,
  "And the hunt is drawing near;
Devils that Paradise disowned;
  They know that I am here.

"And there, O God, a hound gives tongue,
  And great hounds quarter dim."—
The saint's hands to his body clung,
  He knew they came for him.

Then close at hand the horn was loud,
  Like Peter's cock of old,
For joy that Peter's soul was cowed,
  And Jesus' body sold.

Then terribly the hounds in cry
    Gave answer to the horn;
The saint in terror turned to fly
    Before his flesh was torn.

After his body came the hounds,
    After the hounds the horse;
Their running crackled with the sounds
    Of fire that runs in gorse.

The saint's breath failed, but still they came:
    The hunter cheered them on;
Even as a wind that blows a flame
    In the vigil of St. John.

And as St. Withiel's terror grew
    The crying of the pack
Bayed nearer, as though terror drew
    Those grip teeth to his back.

No hope was in his soul, no stay,
    Nothing but screaming will
To save his terror-stricken clay
    Before the hounds could kill.

The laid corn tripped, the bramble caught,
    He stumbled on the stones,
The thorn that scratched him, to his thought,
    Was hell's teeth at his bones.

His legs seemed bound as in a dream,
    The wet earth held his feet,
He screamed aloud as rabbits scream
    Before the stoat's teeth meet.

A black thing struck him on the brow,
  A blackness loomed and waved;
It was a tree. He caught a bough
  And scrambled up it, saved.

Saved for the moment, as he thought,
  He pressed against the bark:
The hell-hounds missed the thing they sought,
  They quartered in the dark.

They panted underneath the tree,
  They quartered to the call,
The hunter cried, "Yoi doit, go see!"
  His death-horn blew a fall.

Now up, now down, the hell-hounds went
  With soft feet padding wide;
They tried, but could not hit the scent,
  However hard they tried.

Then presently the horn was blown,
  The hounds were called away,
The hoof-beats glittered on the stone
  And trotted on the brae.

The saint gat strength, but with it came
  A horror of his fear,
Anguish at having failed, and shame,
  And sense of judgment near.

Anguish at having left his charge
  And having failed his trust,
At having flung his sword and targe
  To save his body's dust.

He clambered down the saving tree;
    "I am unclean," he cried.
"Christ died upon a tree for me,
    I used a tree to hide.

"The hell-hounds bayed about the cross,
    And tore his clothes apart,
But Christ was gold and I am dross,
    And mud is in my heart."

He stood in anguish in the field;
    A little wind blew by,
The dead leaves dropped, the great stars wheeled
    Their squadrons in the sky.

"Lord, I will try again," he said,
    "Though all hell's devils tear.
This time I will not be afraid
    And what is sent I'll dare."

He set his face against the slope
    Until he topped the brae;
Courage had healed his fear, and hope
    Had put his shame away.

And then, far off, a quest-note ran,
    A feathering hound replied:
The hounds still drew the night for man
    Along that countryside.

Then one by one the hell-hounds spoke
    And still the horn made cheer;
Then the full devil-chorus woke
    To fill the saint with fear.

He knew that they were after him
   To hunt him till he fell;
He turned and fled into the dim,
   And after him came hell.

Over the stony wold he went,
   Through thorns and over quags;
The bloodhounds cried upon the scent,
   They ran like rutting stags.

And when the saint looked round, he saw
   Red eyes intently strained,
The bright teeth in the grinning jaw,
   And running shapes that gained.

Uphill, downhill, with failing breath,
   He ran to save his skin,
Like one who knocked the door of death,
   Yet dared not enter in.

Then water gurgled in the night,
   Dark water lay in front,
The saint saw bubbles running bright;
   The huntsman cheered his hunt.

The saint leaped far into the stream
   And struggled to the shore.
The hunt died like an evil dream,
   A strange land lay before.

He waded to a glittering land,
   With brighter light than ours,
The water ran on silver sand
   By yellow water-flowers.

The fishes nosed the stream to rings
　　As petals floated by,
The apples were like orbs of kings
　　Against a glow of sky.

On cool and steady stalks of green
　　The outland flowers grew,
The ghost-flower, silver like a queen,
　　The queen-flower streakt with blue.

The king-flower, crimson on his stalk,
　　With frettings in his crown,
The peace-flower purple, from the chalk,
　　The flower that loves the down.

Lilies like thoughts, roses like words
　　In the sweet brain of June;
The bees there, like the stock-dove birds,
　　Breathed all the air with croon.

Purple and golden hung the plums.
　　Like slaves bowed down with gems
The peach-trees were; sweet-scented gums
　　Oozed clammy from their stems.

And birds of every land were there,
　　Like flowers that sang and flew;
All beauty that makes singing fair
　　That sunny garden knew.

For all together sang with throats
　　So tuned, that the intense
Colour and odour pearled the notes
　　And passed into the sense.

And as the saint drew near, he heard
  The birds talk, each to each,
The fire-bird to the glory-bird;
  He understood their speech.

One said, "The saint was terrified
  Because the hunters came."
Another said, "The bloodhounds cried
  And all their eyes were flame."

Another said, "No shame to him,
  For mortal men are blind,
They cannot see beyond the grim
  Into the peace behind."

Another sang, "They cannot know,
  Unless we give the clue,
The power that waits in them below
  The thing they are to do."

Another sang: "They never guess
  That deep within them stand
Courage and peace and loveliness,
  Wisdom and skill of hand."

Another sang, "Sing, brothers; come,
  Make beauty in the air;
The saint is shamed with martyrdom
  Beyond his strength to bear.

"Sing, brothers, every bird that flies!"
  They stretcht their throats to sing,
With the sweetness known in Paradise
  When the bells of heaven ring.

"Open the doors, good saint," they cried,
　"Pass deeper to your soul;
There is a spirit in your side
　That hell cannot control.

"Open the doors to let him in,
　That beauty with the sword;
The hounds are silly shapes of sin.
　They shrivel at a word.

"Come, saint!" and as they sang, the air
　Shone with the shapes of flame,
Bird after bright bird glittered there,
　Crying aloud they came.

A rush of brightness and delight,
　White as the snow in drift,
The fire-bird and the glory-bright,
　Most beautiful, most swift.

Sweeping aloft to show the way
　And singing as they flew,
Many and glittering as the spray
　When windy seas are blue.

So cheerily they rushed, so strong
　Their sweep was through the flowers,
The saint was swept into their song
　And gloried in their powers.

He sang, and leaped into the stream
　And struggled to the shore;
The garden faded like a dream,
　A darkness lay before.

Darkness with glimmery light forlorn
  And quavering hounds in quest,
A huntsman blowing on a horn,
  And lost things not at rest.

He saw the huntsman's hood show black
  Against the greying east,
He heard him hollo to the pack
  And horn them to the feast.

He heard the bloodhounds come to cry
  And settle to the scent,
The black horse made the hoof-casts fly,
  The sparks flashed up the bent.

The saint stood still until they came
  Baying to ring him round;
A horse whose flecking foam was flame,
  And hound on yelling hound.

And jaws that dripped with bitter fire
  Snarled at the saint to tear.
Pilled hell-hounds, balder than the geier,
  Leaped round him everywhere.

St. Withiel let the hell-hounds rave.
  He cried, "Now, in this place,
Climb down, you huntsman of the grave,
  And let me see your face.

"Climb down, you huntsman out of hell,
  And show me what you are.
The judge has stricken on the bell,
  Now answer at the bar."

The baying of the hounds fell still,
   Their jaws' salt fire died.
The wind of morning struck in chill
   Along that countryside.

The blackness of the horse was shrunk,
   His sides seemed ribbed and old.
The rider, hooded like a monk,
   Was trembling with the cold.

The rider bowed as though with pain;
   Then clambered down and stood,
The thin thing that the frightened brain
   Had fed with living blood.

"Show me.   What are you?" said the saint.
   A hollow murmur spoke.
"This, Lord," it said; a hand moved faint
   And drew aside the cloak.

A Woman Death that palsy shook
   Stood sick and dwindling there;
Her fingers were a bony crook
   And blood was on her hair.

"Stretch out your hands and sign the Cross,"
   Was all St. Withiel said.
The bloodhounds moaned upon the moss,
   The Woman Death obeyed.

Whimpering with pain, she made the sign.
   "Go, devil-hag," said he,
"Beyond all help of bread and wine,
   Beyond all land and sea.

"Into the ice, into the snow,
  Where Death himself is stark.
Out, with your hounds about you, go,
  And perish in the dark."

They dwindled as the mist that fades
  At coming of the sun,
Like rags of stuff that fire abrades,
  They withered and were done.

The cock, that scares the ghost from earth,
  Crowed as they dwindled down;
The red sun, happy in his girth,
  Strode up above the town.

Sweetly above the sunny wold
  The bells of churches rang;
The sheep-bells clinked within the fold,
  And the larks went up and sang.

Sang for the setting free of men
  From devils that destroyed.
The lark, the robin and the wren,
  They joyed and over-joyed.

The chats, that harbour in the whin,
  Their little sweet throats swelled,
The blackbird and the thrush joined in,
  The missel-thrush excelled.

Till round the saint the singing made
  A beauty in the air,
An ecstasy that cannot fade
  But is forever there.

CAP ON HEAD

A TALE OF THE O'NEILL

O'NEILL took ship, O'Neill set sail,
    And left his wife ashore
In the foursquare castle like a jail
    Between the Mull and the Gore.

Many a month he stayed away,
    His lady sorrowed long;
She heard the tide come twice a day
    And the sea-lark at his song;

She watched the sun go down in the west,
    And another day begin,
At nights she made her mate a nest
    But no mate came therein.

———————

One night, a red light burned at sea,
    A ship came in to port,
A foot stirred and the horn was blown
    Within the outer court.

It was all dark, save up the brae,
    The dead moon wore her heel,
The watchman called, "Who's there the day?"
    A voice said, " The O'Neill."

The watchman flung the great gate back,
    "Come in, Lord, to your own."
O'Neill stood huddled up in black,
    Upon the threshold stone.

White as a riser from the dead
   He passed the lintel post.
"God spare us, Lord," the watchman said,
   "I thought you were a ghost.

"I never heard you come ashore,
   And, look your ship is gone.
Are all our fellows dead, my lord,
   That you should come alone?"

O'Neill stood grinning in the porch
   A little breathing space;
The redness blowing from the torch
   Put colour in his face.

"I've left my ship behind," he said,
   "To join the Scotch king's fleet.
I've left my men behind," he said,
   "To haul on her fore-sheet.

"I have come home all alone," he said,
   "In a country ship from sea.
Let my lady know the news," he said,
   "Then open here to me."

Then lights were lit and men gave hail
   And welcomed him ashore;
The wife was glad within that jail
   Between the Mull and the Gore.

O'Neill went swimming in the sea
   And hunting up the glen;
No one could swim or ride as he
   Of all the sons of men.

His wife went happy in the lane,
   And singing in the tower;
The sweet of having him again
   Had ended all the sour.

But Kate, an old crone muttering dark
   About that windy place,
Did not rejoice: she said, "I mark
   O'Neill has fal'n from grace.

"He has been under the dark star
   Since when he went away.
Men think that when they wander far
   The black thing becomes grey.

"He has been dipped in the strange vat
   And dyed with the strange dye,
And then the black thing, what is that
   That dogs him, going by?

"A dog thing, black, goes padding past
   Forever at his heel:
God help us all to peace at last,
   I fear for the O'Neill.

"His teeth show when the Host does come
   To comfort dying men,
And in the chapel he is dumb,
   He never says Amen."

She would not speak with the O'Neill,
   But when he crossed her path
She prayed, as tremblers do that feel
   The devil in his wrath.

And so the Time went by, whose hand
  Upheaves the lives of men,
The cuckoo left his burning land
  To toll along the glen.

So loud the thrushes sang that spring,
  So rich the hawthorn was,
The air was like a living thing
  Between the sky and the grass.

O'Neill's wife bore a little son
  And set him on her knee;
He grew apace to romp and run
  And dabble in the sea.

But one thing strange about the child
  The neighbors noted there:
That, even if the winds were mild,
  His head was never bare.

His father made him wear a cap
  At all times, night and day,
Bound round his forehead with a strap
  To keep the cold away.

And up and down the little lad
  Went singing at his game:
Men marvelled at the grace he had
  To make the wild birds tame.

Men marvelled at the joy he took
  And at the things he said,
And at the beauty of his look,
  This little Cap on Head.

And when the nights were dark between
  The new moon and the old,
And fires were lit, and winds blew keen,
  And old wives' tales were told,

This little son would scramble near
  Beside his mother's place,
To listen to the tale and peer
  With firelight on his face.

O'Neill would gather to the glow
  With great eyes glittering fierce;
Old Kate would shake to see him so
  And cross herself from curse.

It fell about hay-harvest time,
  When the Lammas floods were out,
A ship all green with water-slime
  Stood in and went about,

And anchored off the bight of sand,
  And swam there like a seal,
With a banner of the bloody hand,
  The flag of the O'Neill.

Then there was cheering in the court
  And hurrying to the beach:
"A ship!" they cried, "A ship in port,
  Brought up in Castle Reach.

"It is our ship. They are our men
  There, coiling up the sheet;
It is our ship come home agen
  From out the Scotch King's fleet.

"And who's the noble in the boat
　Comes rowing through the sea?
His colours are the O'Neill coat,
　But what O'Neill is he?"

O'Neill was in his turret tower,
　With writings red and black;
Kate crossed herself to see him glower
　That tide the ship came back.

He looked long at the anchored ship,
　And at the coming boat;
The devil writhelled up his lip,
　And snickered in his throat.

He strode the room and bit his nails,
　He bit his flesh with rage,
As maddened felons do in jails,
　And rats do in a cage.

He looked at Kate, who crossed her breast,
　He heard them cheer below:
He said, "The wicked cannot rest,
　And now I have to go."

They saw him hurry up the green
　And on into the rain;
Beyond the brae he was not seen:
　He was not seen again.

O'Neill's wife went to watch the boat
　Come driving to the sand:
The noble in the O'Neill coat
　Stood up and waved his hand.

"That is O'Neill!" the clansmen cried,
　"Or else his very twin.
How came he to the ship?" they cried.
　"Just now he was within."

"It is O'Neill," the lady said,
　"And that's his ship returned.
A woman's life's a school," she said,
　"Where bitter things are learned."

O'Neill called to her through his tears,
　"The bitter days are past.
I've prayed for this for seven years,
　Now here I am at last."

Then, as the boat's bows cut the strand,
　Among the slipping foam,
He sprang to take his lady's hand,
　He said, "I have come home."

His lady fainted like the dead,
　Beside the slipping sea.
"This is O'Neill," the servants said,
　"What is that other he?"

"Master," they said, "where have you been
　These seven years and more?"
"I've served the Scottish King and Queen,
　Along the Scottish shore."

"Master," they said, "Another came
　So like in voice and face
To you, we thought it was the same,
　And so he took your place.

"These seven years he's ruled us here,
  While you were still at sea,
And that's his son that's coming here:
  Look, Master, that is he."

O'Neill took off the wee boy's cap
  And ruffled through his hair;
He said, "A young tree full of sap,
  A good shoot growing fair."

He turned the hair for men to see
  And swallowed down his tears;
He said, "The gods be good to me,
  The boy has devil's ears."

He took the young child by the heels
  And broke him, head and breast:
The red hand ridded the O'Neills
  That cuckoo in the nest.

O'Neill flung out the little limbs
  To drift about the bay:
"Watch, fellows, if he sinks or swims,"
  Was all they heard him say.

He said, "The wicked cannot rest
  And now I have to go."
He set his ship's head north and west
  And stood into the flow.

The ship went shining like a seal
  And dimmed into the rain—
And no man saw the great O'Neill,
  Nor heard of him again.

SONNETS

Like bones the ruins of the cities stand,
Like skeletons and skulls with ribs and eyes
Strewn in the saltness of the desert sand
Carved with the unread record of Kings' lies.

Once they were strong with soldiers, loud with voices,
The markets clattered as the carts drove through,
Where now the jackal in the moon rejoices
And the still asp draws death along the dew.

There at the gates the market men paid toll
In bronze and silver pennies long worn thin
Wine was a silver penny for a bowl
Women they had there, and the moon and sin.

And looking from his tower the watchman saw
Green fields for miles, the roads, the great king's law.

———

Now they are gone with all their songs and sins,
Women and men, to dust; their copper penny,
Of living, spent, among these dusty inns;
The glittering One made level with the many.

Their speech is gone, none speaks it, none can read
The pictured writing of their conqueror's march
The dropping plaster of a fading screed
Ceils with its mildews the decaying arch.

The fields are sand, the streets are fallen stones
Nothing is bought or sold there, nothing spoken,
The sand hides all, the wind that blows it moans,
Blowing more sand until the plinth is broken,

Day in, day out, no other utterance falls;
Only the sand, pit-pitting on the walls.

None knows what overthrew that city's pride.
Some say, the spotted pestilence arose
And smote them to the marrow, that they died
Till every pulse was dusty; no man knows.

Some say, that foreign Kings with all their hosts,
Sieged it with mine and tower till it fell
So that the sword shred shrieking flesh from ghosts
Till every street was empty; who can tell?

Some think, that in the fields, or in the pit,
Out of the light, in filth, among the rotten,
Insects like sands in number, swift as wit,
Famined the city dead; it is forgotten.

Only the city's bones stand, gaunt in air,
Pocked by the pitting sandspecks everywhere.

So shall we be; so will our cities lie,
Unknown beneath the grasses of the summer,
Walls without roofs, naves open to the sky,
Doors open to the wind, the only comer.

And men will grub the ruins, eyes will peer,
Fingers will grope for pennies, brains will tire
To chronicle the skills we practised here,
While still we breathed the wind and trod the mire.

O, like the ghost at dawn, scared by the cock,
Let us make haste, to let the spirit dive
Deep in self's sea, until the deeps unlock
The depths and sunken gold of being alive

Till, though our Many pass, a Something stands
Aloft through Time that covers all with sands.

THE PASSING STRANGE

Out of the earth to rest or range
Perpetual in perpetual change
The unknown passing through the strange.

Water and saltness held together
To tread the dust and stand the weather
And plough the field and stretch the tether.

To pass the wine cup and be witty,
Water the sands and build the city
Slaughter like devils and have pity,

Be red with rage and pale with lust,
Make beauty come, make peace, make trust,
Water and saltness mixed with dust;

Drive over earth, swim under sea,
Fly in the eagle's secrecy,
Guess where the hidden comets be;

Know all the deathy seeds that still
Queen Helen's beauty, Cæsar's will,
And slay them even as they kill,

Fashion an altar for a rood,
Defile a continent with blood,
And watch a brother starve for food;

Love like a madman, shaking, blind
Till self is burnt into a kind
Possession of another mind;

Brood upon beauty till the grace
Of beauty with the holy face
Brings peace into the bitter place;

Probe in the lifeless granites, scan
The stars for hope, for guide, for plan;
Live as a woman or a man;

Fasten to lover or to friend
Until the heart break at the end
The break of death that cannot mend

Then to lie useless, helpless, still
Down in the earth, in dark, to fill
The roots of grass or daffodil.

Down in the earth, in dark, alone,
A mockery of the ghost in bone,
The strangeness, passing the unknown.

Time will go by, that outlasts clocks,
Dawn in the thorps will rouse the cocks
Sunset be glory on the rocks

But it, the thing, will never heed
Even the rootling from the seed
Thrusting to suck it for its need.

Since moons decay and suns decline
How else should end this life of mine?
Water and saltness are not wine.

But in the darkest hour of night
When even the foxes peer for sight
The byre-cock crows; he feels the light.

So, in this water mixed with dust,
The byre-cock spirit crows from trust
That death will change because it must,

For all things change, the darkness changes,
The wandering spirits change their ranges,
The corn is gathered to the granges.

The corn is sown again, it grows;
The stars burn out, the darkness goes.
The rhythms change, they do not close.

They change, and we, who pass like foam,
Like dust blown through the streets of Rome,
Change ever, too; we have no home,

Only a beauty, only a power,
Sad in the fruit, bright in the flower,
Endlessly erring for its hour

But gathering, as we stray, a sense
Of Life, so lovely and intense,
It lingers when we wander hence.

That those who follow feel behind
Their backs, when all before is blind,
Our joy, a rampart to the mind.

ANIMULA

This is the place, this house beside the sea,
This was the setting where they played their parts
Two men, who knew them all, have talked to me.
Beauty she had, and all had passionate hearts.

I write this in the window where she sat
Two fields, all green with summer, lie below
Then the grey sea, at thought, cloud-coloured, flat,
Wind-dappled from the glen, the tide at flow.

Her portrait and her husband's hang together
One on each side the fire; it is close:
The tree-tops toss; it is a change of weather;
They were most lovely and unhappy, those

That married pair and he who loved too well;
This was the door by which they entered hell.

This, is a drawing of her as a child,
This, is she wed; the faces are the same,
Only, the beauty of the babe is wild;
The woman's beauty has been broken tame.

Witty, bright, gentle, earnest, with great eyes,
Dark hair in heaps, pure colour, lips that smile;
Beauty that is more wisdom than the wise
Lived in this woman for a little while.

Dressed in that beauty that our mothers wore,
(So touching now), she looks out of the frame
With stag-like eyes, that wept till they were sore
Many's the time, till she was broken tame.

Witty, bright, gentle, earnest, even so:
Destiny calls and spirits come and go.

This, is her husband in his youth; and this
Is he in manhood; this, is he in age:
There is a devil in those eyes of his,
A glittering devil, restless in his cage.

A grand man, with a beauty and a pride
A manner and a power and a fire
With beaks of vultures eating at his side
The great brain mad with unfulfilled desire.

"With grand ideas," they say; tall, wicked, proud,
Cold, cruel, bitter, clever, dainty, skilled;
Splendid to see, a head above the crowd,
Splendid with every strength, yet unfulfilled.
Cutting himself (and all those near) with hate
From that sharp mind which should have shaped a state.

And many years ago I saw the third
Bowed in old age and mad with misery
Mad with the bright eyes of the eagle bird;
Burning his heart at fires of memory.

He stood behind a chair and bent and muttered
Grand still, grey, sunburnt, bright with mad eyes brown,
Burning, though dying, like a torch that guttered
That once had lit Queen Helen through the town.

I only saw him once: I saw him go
Leaning uphill his body to the rain
Too good a man for life to punish so
Theirs were the pride and passion, his the pain.

His old coat flapped: the little children turned
To see him pass, that passionate age that burned.

"I knew them well, all three," the old man said;
"He was an unused force and she a child.
She caught him with her beauty, being a maid.
The thought that she had trapped him drove him wild.

He would not work with others, could not rest,
And nothing here could use him or engage him
Yet here he stayed with devils in his breast
To blast the woman who had dared to cage him.

Then, when the scholar came, it made the three,
She turned to him and he, he turned to her.
They both were saints: elopement could not be:
So here they stayed, and passion plied the spur.

Then the men fought, and later she was found
In that green pool beyond the headland, drowned.

They carried her drowned body up the grass
Here to the house, they laid it on the bed
(This very bed, where I have slept, it was)
The scholar begged to see her, being dead.

The husband walked downstairs to see him there
Begging to see her as one asks an alms
He spat at him and cut his cheek-bone bare
"There's pay," he said, "my poet, for your psalms."

And then they fought together at the door
Biting each other, like two dogs, while she
Lay dead, poor woman, dripping on the floor
Out of her hair the death-drops of the sea.

Later, they fought whenever they might meet
In church, or in the fields, or in the street."

Up, on the hill, another aged man
Remembered them. He said, "they were afraid.
They feared to end the passions they began.
They held the cards and yet they never played.

He should have broken from her at all cost.
She should have loved her lover and gone free.
They all held winning cards and yet they lost
So two were wrecked and one drowned in the sea.

Some harshness or some law, or else some fear
Stifled their souls: God help us, when we know
Certainly, certain things, the way is clear.
And yet, they paid, and one respects them, so.

Perhaps they were too fine. I know not, I.
Men must have mercy, being ripe to die."

So this old house of mourning was the stage
(This house and those green fields) for all that woe.
There are her books, her writing on the page,
In those chocked beds she made the flowers grow.

Most desolate it is, the rain is pouring
The trees all toss and drip and scatter evil,
The floods are out, the waterfall is roaring,
The bar is mad with many a leaping devil.

And in this house the wind goes whining wild
The door blows open, till I think to see
That delicate sweet woman like a child
Standing with great dark stag's eyes watching me.

Watching as though her sorrow might make plain
(Had I but wit) the meaning of such pain.

I wonder if she sang in this old room.
Ah, never; no; they tell me that she stood
For hours together staring into gloom
Out of the prison bars of flesh and blood.

So, when the ninth wave drowned her, haply she
Wakened, with merging senses, till she blent
Into the joy and colour of the sea
One with the purpose of the element.

And there, perhaps, she cannot feel the woe
Passed in this rotting house, but runs like light
Over the billows where the clippers go,
One with the blue sea's pureness of delight.

Laughing, perhaps, at that old woe of hers
Chained in the cage with fellow prisoners.

He died in that lone cottage near the sea.
In the grey morning when the tide was turning,
The wards of life slipt back and set him free
From cares of meat and dress, from joys and yearning.

Then, like an old man gathering strength, he strayed
Over the beach, and strength came into him
Beauty that never threatened nor betrayed
Made bright the eyes that sorrow had made dim

So that upon that stretch of barren sand
He knew his dreams; he saw her beauty run
With Sorrowful Beauty, laughing, hand in hand,
He heard the trumpets blow in Avalon.

He saw the golden statue stretching down
The wreath, for him, of roses, in a crown.

They say that as her husband lay a-dying
He clamoured for a chain to beat the hound.
They say that all the garden rang with crying
That came out of the air, out of the ground,

Out of the waste that was his soul, may be,
Out of the running wolf-hound of his soul,
That had been kennelled in and now broke free
Out to the moors where stags go, past control.

All through his life his will had kennelled him
Now he was free, and with a hackling fell
He snarled out of the body to the dim
To run the spirits with the hounds of hell.

To run forever at the quarry gone,
The uncaught thing a little further on.

So, one by one, Time took them to his keeping
Those broken lanterns that had held his fire,
Dust went to dust and flesh had time for sleeping,
And soul, the stag, escaped the hound desire.

And now, perhaps, the memory of their hate
Has passed from them and they are friends again
Laughing at all the troubles of this state
Where men and women work each other pain.

And in that wind that runs along the glen
Beating at cottage doors, they may go by,
Exulting now, and helping sorrowing men
To do some little good before they die.

For from these ploughed-up souls the spirit brings
Harvest at last, and sweet from bitter things.

THE LEMMINGS

Once in a hundred years the Lemmings come
Westward, in search of food, over the snow,
Westward, until the salt sea drowns them dumb,
Westward, till all are drowned, those Lemmings go.

Once, it is thought, there was a westward land,
(Now drowned) where there was food for those starved things,
And memory of the place has burnt its brand
In the little brains of all the Lemming Kings.

Perhaps, long since, there was a land beyond
Westward from death, some city, some calm place,
Where one could taste God's quiet and be fond
With the little beauty of a human face;

But now the land is drowned, yet still we press
Westward, in search, to death, to nothingness.

166

FORGET

Forget all these, the barren fool in power,
The madman in command, the jealous O,
The bitter world biting its bitter hour,
The cruel now, the happy long ago.

Forget all these, for, though they truly hurt,
Even to the soul, they are not lasting things,
Men are no gods; we tread the city dirt,
But in our souls we can be queens and kings.

And I, O Beauty, O divine white wonder,
On whom my dull eyes, blind to all else, peer,
Have you for peace, that not the whole war's thunder
Nor the world's wreck, can threat or take from here.

So you remain, though all man's passionate seas
Roar their blind tides, I can forget all these.

ON GROWING OLD

Be with me Beauty for the fire is dying,
My dog and I are old, too old for roving,
Man, whose young passion sets the spindrift flying
Is soon too lame to march, too cold for loving.

I take the book and gather to the fire,
Turning old yellow leaves; minute by minute,
The clock ticks to my heart; a withered wire
Moves a thin ghost of music in the spinet.

I cannot sail your seas, I cannot wander,
Your cornland, nor your hill-land nor your valleys,
Ever again, nor share the battle yonder
Where the young knight the broken squadron rallies.

Only stay quiet while my mind remembers
The beauty of fire from the beauty of embers.

Beauty, have pity, for the strong have power
The rich their wealth, the beautiful their grace
Summer of man its sunlight and its flower
Spring time of man all April in a face.

Only, as in the jostling in the Strand,
Where the mob thrusts or loiters or is loud
The beggar with the saucer in his hand
Asks only a penny from the passing crowd,

So, from this glittering world with all its fashion
Its fire and play of men, its stir, its march,
Let me have wisdom, Beauty, wisdom and passion,
Bread to the soul, rain where the summers parch.

Give me but these, and though the darkness close
Even the night will blossom as the rose

LYRIC

Give me a light that I may see her,
Give me a grace that I may be her,
Give me a clue that I may find her,
Whose beauty shews the brain behind her.
Stars and women and running rivers
And sunny water where a shadow shivers,
And the little brooks that lift the grasses
And April flowers are where she passes.
And all things good and all things kind
Are glimmerings coming from her mind
And in the may a blackbird sings
Against her very heartë springs.

RIGHT ROYAL

An hour before the race they talked together
A pair of lovers in the mild March weather,
Charles Cothill and the golden lady, Em.
Beautiful England's hands had fashioned them.

He was from Sleins, that manor up the Lithe;
Riding the Downs had made his body blithe;
Stalwart he was, and springy, hardened, swift,
Able for perfect speed with perfect thrift,
Man to the core yet moving like a lad.
Dark honest eyes with merry gaze he had,
A fine firm mouth, and wind-tan on his skin.
He was to ride and ready to begin.
He was to ride Right Royal, his own horse,
In the English Chaser's Cup on Compton Course.

Under the pale coat reaching to his spurs
One saw his colours, which were also hers,
Narrow alternate bars of blue and white
Blue as the speedwell's eye and silver bright.

What with hard work and waiting for the race,
Trouble and strain were marked upon his face;
Men would have said that something worried him.

She was a golden lady, dainty, trim,
As like the love time as laburnum blossom.
Mirth, truth and goodness harboured in her bosom.

Pure colour and pure contour and pure grace
Made the sweet marvel of her singing face;

She was the very may-time that comes in
When hawthorns bud and nightingales begin.
To see her tread the red-tippet daisies white
In the green fields all golden with delight,
Was to believe Queen Venus come again,
She was as dear as sunshine after rain;
Such loveliness this golden lady had.

All lovely things and pure things made her glad,
But most she loved the things her lover loved,
The windy Downlands where the kestrels roved,
The sea of grasses that the wind runs over
Where blundering beetles drunken from the clover
Stumble about the startled passer-by.

There on the great grass underneath the sky
She loved to ride with him for hours on hours,
Smelling the seasoned grass and those small flowers,
Milkworts and thymes, that grow upon the Downs.
There from a chalk edge they would see the towns:
Smoke above trees, by day, or spires of churches
Gleaming with swinging wind-cocks on their perches.
Or windows flashing in the light, or trains
Burrowing below white smoke across the plains.
By night, the darkness of the valley set
With scattered lights to where the ridges met
And three great glares making the heaven dun,
Oxford and Wallingford and Abingdon.
"Dear, in an hour," said Charles, "the race begins.
Before I start I must confess my sins.
For I have sinned, and now it troubles me."

"I saw that you were sad," said Emily.

"Before I speak," said Charles, "I must premise.
You were not here to help me to be wise,

And something happened, difficult to tell.
Even if I sinned, I feel I acted well,
From inspiration, mad as that may seem.
Just at the grey of dawn I had a dream.

It was the strangest dream I ever had.
It was the dream that drove me to be mad.

I dreamed I stood upon the race-course here,
Watching a blinding rainstorm blowing clear,
And as it blew away I said aloud,
'That rain will make soft going on the ploughed.'
And instantly I saw the whole great course,
The grass, the brooks, the fences toppt with gorse,
Gleam in the sun; and all the ploughland shone
Blue, like a marsh, though now the rain had gone.
And in my dream I said, 'That plough will be
Terrible work for some, but not for me.
Not for Right Royal.'
       And a voice said, 'No
Not for Right Royal.'
       And I looked, and lo
There was Right Royal, speaking, at my side.
The horse's very self, and yet his hide
Was like, what shall I say? like pearl on fire,
A white soft glow of burning that did twire
Like soft white-heat with every breath he drew.
A glow, with utter brightness running through;
Most splendid, though I cannot make you see.

His great crest glittered as he looked at me
Criniered with spitting sparks; he stamped the ground
All cock and fire, trembling like a hound,
And glad of me, and eager to declare
His horse's mind.

And I was made aware
That, being a horse, his mind could only say
Few things to me. He said, 'It is my day,
My day, to-day; I shall not have another.'

And as he spoke he seemed a younger brother
Most near, and yet a horse, and then he grinned
And tossed his crest and crinier to the wind

And looked down to the Water with an eye
All fire of soul to gallop dreadfully.

All this was strange, but then a stranger thing
Came afterwards. I woke all shivering
With wonder and excitement, yet with dread
Lest the dream meant that Royal should be dead,
Lest he had died and come to tell me so.
I hurried out; no need to hurry, though;
There he was shining like a morning star.
Now hark. You know how cold his manners are,
Never a whinny for his dearest friend.
To-day he heard me at the courtyard end,
He left his breakfast with a shattering call,
A View Halloo, and, swinging in his stall,
Ran up to nuzzle me with signs of joy.
It staggered Harding and the stable-boy.
And Harding said, 'What's come to him to-day?
He must have had a dream he beat the bay.'

Now that was strange; and, what was stranger, this.
I know he tried to say those words of his,
'It is my day'; and Harding turned to me,
'It is his day to-day, that's plain to see.'
Right Royal nuzzled at me as he spoke.
That staggered me. I felt that I should choke.

It came so pat upon my unsaid thought,
I asked him what he meant.
                    He answered 'Naught.
It only came into my head to say.
But there it is. To-day's Right Royal's day.'

That was the dream. I cannot put the glory
With which it filled my being, in a story.
No one can tell a dream.
                    Now to confess.
The dream made daily life a nothingness,
Merely a mould which white-hot beauty fills,
Pure from some source of passionate joys and skills.
And being flooded with my vision thus,
Certain of winning, puffed and glorious,
Walking upon this earth-top like a king,
My judgment went. I did a foolish thing,
I backed myself to win with all I had.

Now that it's done I see that it was mad,
But still, I had to do it, feeling so.
That is the full confession; now you know."

SHE
The thing is done, and being done, must be.
You cannot hedge. Would you had talked with me
Before you plunged. But there, the thing is done.

HE
Do not exaggerate the risks I run.
Right Royal was a bad horse in the past,
A rogue, a cur, but he is cured at last;
For I was right, his former owner wrong,
He is a game good chaser going strong.
He and my lucky star may pull me through.

SHE
O grant they may; but think what's racing you,
Think for a moment what his chances are
Against Sir Lopez, Soyland, Kubbadar.

HE
You said you thought Sir Lopez past his best.
I do, myself.

SHE
                        But there are all the rest.
Peterkinooks, Red Ember, Counter Vair,
And then Grey Glory and the Irish mare.

HE
She's scratched. The rest are giving me a stone.
Unless the field hides something quite unknown
I stand a chance. The going favours me.
The ploughland will be bogland certainly,
After this rain. If Royal keeps his nerve,
If no one cannons me at jump or swerve,
I stand a chance. And though I dread to fail,
This passionate dream that drives me like a sail
Runs in my blood, and cries, that I shall win.

SHE
Please Heaven you may; but now (for me) begin
Again the horrors that I cannot tell,
Horrors that made my childhood such a hell,
Watching my Father near the gambler's grave
Step after step, yet impotent to save.

You do not know, I never let you know,
The horror of those days of long ago
When Father raced to ruin. Every night

After my Mother took away the light
For weeks before each meeting, I would see
Horrible horses looking down on me
Laughing and saying "We shall beat your Father."
Then when the meetings came I used to gather
Close up to Mother, and we used to pray.
"O God, for Christ's sake, let him win to-day."

And then we had to watch for his return,
Craning our necks to see if we could learn,
Before he entered, what the week had been.

Now I shall look on such another scene
Of waiting on the race-chance. For to-day,
Just as I did with Father, I shall say
"Yes, he'll be beaten by a head, or break
A stirrup leather at the wall, or take
The brook too slow, and, then, all will be lost."

Daily, in mind, I saw the Winning Post,
The Straight, and all the horses' glimmering forms
Rushing between the railings' yelling swarms,
My Father's colours leading. Every day,
Closing my eyes, I saw them die away,
In the last strides, and lose, lose by a neck,
Lose by an inch, but lose, and bring the wreck
A day's march nearer. Now begins again
The agony of waiting for the pain.
The agony of watching ruin come
Out of man's dreams to overwhelm a home.

Go now, my dear. Before the race is due,
We'll meet again, and then I'll speak with you.

In a race-course box behind the Stand
Right Royal shone from a strapper's hand.

A big dark bay with a restless tread,
Fetlock deep in a wheat-straw bed;
A noble horse of a nervy blood,
By O Mon Roi out of Rectitude.
Something quick in his eye and ear
Gave a hint that he might be queer.
In front, he was all to a horseman's mind,
Some thought him a trifle light behind.
By two good points might his rank be known,
A beautiful head and a Jumping Bone.
He had been the hope of Sir Button Budd,
Who bred him there at the Fletchings stud,
But the Fletchings jockey had flogged him cold
In a narrow thing as a two-year-old.
After that, with his sulks and swerves,
Dread of the crowd and fits of nerves,
Like a wastrel bee who makes no honey
He had hardly earned his entry money.

Liking him still, though he failed at racing,
Sir Button trained him for steeple-chasing.
He jumped like a stag, but his heart was cowed;
Nothing would make him face the crowd;
When he reached the Straight where the crowds began
He would make no effort for any man.

Sir Button sold him, Charles Cothill bought him,
Rode him to hounds and soothed and taught him.
After two years' care Charles felt assured
That his horse's broken heart was cured,
And the jangled nerves in tune again.
And now, as proud as a King of Spain,
He moved in his box with a restless tread,
His eyes like sparks in his lovely head,
Ready to run between the roar

Of the stands that face the Straight once more;
Ready to race, though blown, though beat,
As long as his will could lift his feet,
Ready to burst his heart to pass
Each gasping horse in that street of grass.
John Harding said to his stable-boy,

"Would looks were deeds, for he looks a joy.
He's come on well in the last ten days."
The horse looked up at the note of praise,
He fixed his eye upon Harding's eye,
Then he put all thought of Harding by,
Then his ears went back and he clipped all clean
The manger's well where his oats had been.

John Harding walked to the stable-yard,
His brow was worried with thinking hard.
He thought, "His sire was a Derby winner,
His legs are steel, and he loves his dinner,
And yet of old when they made him race,
He sulked or funked like a real disgrace;
Now for man or horse, I say, it's plain,
That what once he's been, he'll be again.

For all his looks, I'll take my oath
That horse is a cur, and slack as sloth.

He'll funk at a great big field like this,
And the lad won't cure that sloth of his,
He stands no chance, and yet Bungay says
He's been backed all morning a hundred ways.
He was twenty to one, last night, by Heaven:
Twenty to one and now he's seven.
Well, one of these fools whom fortune loves
Has made up his mind to go for the gloves;
But here's Dick Cappell to bring me news."

Dick Cappell came from a London Mews,
His fleshless face was a stretcht skin sheath
For the narrow pear of the skull beneath.
He had cold blue eyes, and a mouth like a slit,
With yellow teeth sticking out from it.
There was no red blood in his lips or skin,
He'd a sinister, hard, sharp soul within.
Perhaps, the thing that he most enjoyed
Was being rude when he felt annoyed.
He sucked his cane, he nodded to John,
He asked, "What's brought your lambkin on?"

John said, "I had meant to ask of you,
Who's backing him, Dick, I hoped you knew."
Dick said, "Pill Stewart has placed the money.
I don't know whose."
                    John said, "That's funny."

"Why funny?" said Dick; but John said naught;
He looked at the horse's legs and thought.
Yet at last he said, "It beats me clean,
But whoever he is, he must be green.
There are eight in this could give him a stone,
And twelve should beat him on form alone.
The lad can ride, but it's more than riding
That will give the bay and the grey a hiding."

Dick sucked his cane and looked at the horse
With "Nothing's certain on Compton Course.
He looks a peach. Have you tried him high?"
John said, "You know him as well as I;
What he has done and what he can do.
He's been ridden to hounds this year or two.
When last he was raced, he made the running,
For a stable companion twice at Sunning.

He was placed, bad third, in the Blowbury Cup
And second at Tew with Kingston up.
He sulked at Folkestone, he funked at Speen,
He baulked at the ditch at Hampton Green,
Nick Kingston thought him a slug and cur,
'You must cut his heart out to make him stir.'
But his legs are iron; he's fine and fit."

Dick said, "Maybe; but he's got no grit.
With to-day's big field, on a course like this,
He will come to grief with that funk of his.
Well. It's queer, to me, that they've brought him on.
It's Kubbadar's race. Good morning, John."

When Dick had gone from the stable-yard,
John wrote a note on a racing card.
He said, "Since Stewart has placed the com.,
It's Mr. Cothill he got it from.
Now why should that nice young man go blind
And back his horse? Has he lost his mind?
Such a nice young fellow, so civil-spoken,
Should have more sense than to get him broken,
For broken he'll be as sure as eggs
If he puts his money on horses' legs.
And to trust to this, who's a nice old thing,
But can no more win than a cow can sing.
Well, they say that wisdom is dearly bought,
A world of pain for a want of thought;
But why should he back what stands no chance,
No more than the Rowley Mile's in France?
Why didn't he talk of it first with me?

Well, Lord, we trainers can let it be,
Why can't these owners abstain the same?
It can't be aught but a losing game.

He'll finish ninth; he'll be forced to sell
His horse, his stud, and his home as well;
He'll lose his lady, and all for this
A daft belief in that horse of his.

It's nothing to me, a man might say,
That a rich young fool should be cast away,
Though what he does with his own, in fine,
Is certainly no concern of mine.
I'm paid to see that his horse is fit,
I can't engage for an owner's wit.
For the heart of a man may love his brother,
But who can be wise to save another?
Souls are our own to save from burning,
We must all learn how, and pay for learning.

And now, by the clock, that bell that went
Was the Saddling Bell for the first event.

Since the time comes close, it will save some swearing
If we get beforehand, and start preparing."

The roads were filled with a drifting crowd,
Many mouth-organs droned aloud,
A couple of lads in scarlet hats,
Yellow trousers and purple spats,
Dragged their banjos, wearily eyeing
Passing brakes full of sportsmen Hi-ing.

Then with a long horn blowing a glory
Came the four-in-hand of the young Lord Tory,
The young Lord's eyes on his leader's ears
And the blood-like team going by to cheers.
Then in a brake came cheerers and hooters
Peppering folk from tin peashooters;

The Green Man's Friendly in bright mauve caps
Followed fast in the Green Man's traps,
The crowd made way for the traps to pass
Then a drum beat up with a blare of brass,
Medical students smart as paint
Sang gay songs of a sad complaint.

A wolf-eyed man who carried a kipe
Whistled as shrill as a man could pipe,
Then paused and grinned with his gaps of teeth
Crying "Here's your colours for Compton Heath,
All the colours of all the starters,
For gentlemen's ties and ladies' garters;
Here you have them, penny a pin,
Buy your colours and see them win.
Here you have them, the favourites' own,
Sir Lopez' colours, the blue-white-roan,
For all the races and what'll win 'em
Real jockey's silk with a pin to pin 'em."

Out of his kipe he sold to many
Bright silk buttons and charged a penny.

A bookie walked with his clerk beside him,
His stool on his shoulders seemed to ride him,
His white top-hat bore a sign which ran
"Your old pal Bunkie the working man."
His clothes were a check of three-inch squares,
"Bright brown and fawn with the pearls in pairs."
Double pearl buttons ran down the side,
The knees were tight and the ankles wide,
A bright, thick chain made of discs of tin
Secured a board from his waist to chin.

The men in the brakes that passed at trot
Read "First past Post" and "Run or Not."

The bookie's face was an angry red,
His eyes seemed rolling inside his head.
His clerk was a lean man, secret, spare,
With thin lips knowing and damp black hair.
A big black bag much weathered with rain
Hung round his neck by a leathered chain.

Seven linked dancers singing a song
Bowed and kicked as they danced along,
The middleman thrust and pulled and squeezed
A concertina to tunes that pleased.
After them, honking, with Hey, Hey, Hey,
Came drivers thrusting to clear the way,
Drivers vexed by the concertina,
Saying "Go bury that d——d hyena."
Drivers dusty with wind-red faces
Leaning out of their driving-places.
The dancers mocked them and called them names:
"Look at our butler," "Drive on, James."
The cars drove past and the dust rose after,
Little boys chased them yelling with laughter,
Clambering on them when they slowed
For a dirty ride down a perch of road.
A dark green car with a smart drab lining
Passed with a stately pair reclining;
Peering walkers standing aside
Saw Soyland's owner pass with his bride,
Young Sir Eustace, biting his lip,
Pressing his chin with his finger-tip,
Nerves on edge, as he could not choose,
From thought of the bets he stood to lose.
His lady, a beauty whom thought made pale,
Prayed from fear that the horse might fail.
A bright brass rod on the motor's bonnet
Carried her husband's colours on it,

Scarlet spots on a field of cream:
She stared ahead in a kind of dream.

Then came cabs from the railway stations,
Carrying men from all the nations,
Olive-skinned French with clipped moustaches,
Almond-eyed like Paris apaches.
Rosy French with their faces shining
From joy of living and love of dining.
Silent Spaniards, merry Italians,
Nobles, commoners, saints, rapscallions;
Russians tense with the quest of truth
That maddens manhood and saddens youth;
Learned Norwegians hale and limber,
Brown from the barques new in with timber.
Oregon men of six feet seven
With backs from Atlas and hearts from Heaven.
Orleans Creoles, ready for duels,
Their delicate ears with scarlet jewels,
Green silk handkerchiefs round their throats,
In from sea with the cotton boats.
Portuguese and Brazilianos,
Men from the mountains, men from the Llanos,
Men from the Pampas, men from the Sierras,
Men from the mines of the Cordilleras,
Men from the flats of the tropic mud
Where the butterfly glints his mail with blood;
Men from the pass where day by day
The sun's heat scales the rocks away;
Men from the hills where night by night
The sheep-bells give the heart delight;
Indians, Lascars and Bengalese.
Greeks from the mainland, Greeks from the seas;
All kinds of bodies, all kinds of faces,
All were coming to see the races,

Coming to see Sir Lopez run
And watch the English having their fun.

The Carib boxer from Hispaniola
Wore a rose in his titled bowler;
He drove a car with a yellow panel,
He went full speed and he drove a channel.

Then came dog-carts and traps and wagons
With hampers of lunches, pies and flagons,
Bucks from city and flash young bloods
With vests "cut saucy" to show their studs,
Hawbuck Towler and Spicey Random
Tooled in style in a rakish tandem.
Blood Dick Haggit and Bertie Askins
Had dancers' skirts on their horses' gaskins;
Crash Pete Snounce with that girl of Dowser's
Drove a horse that was wearing trousers;
The waggonette from The Old Pier Head
Drove to the tune "My Monkey's Dead."

The costermongers as smart as sparrows
Brought their wives in their donkey barrows.
The clean-legged donkeys, clever and cunning,
Their ears cocked forward, their neat feet running,
Their carts and harness flapping with flags,
Were bright as heralds and proud as stags.
And there in pride in the flapping banners
Were the costers' selves in blue bandannas,
And the costers' wives in feathers curling,
And their sons, with their sweet mouth-organs skirling.

And from midst of the road to the roadside shifting
The crowd of the world on foot went drifting,
Standing aside on the trodden grass

To chaff as they let the traffic pass.
Then back they flooded, singing and cheering,
Plodding forward and disappearing,
Up to the course to take their places,
To lunch and gamble and see the races.

The great grand stand, made grey by the weather,
Flaunted colours that tugged their tether;
Tier upon tier the wooden seats
Were packed as full as the London streets
When the King and Queen go by in state.

Click click clack went the turnstile gate;
The orange-sellers cried "Fat and fine
Seville oranges, sweet, like wine:
Twopence apiece, all juice, all juice."
The pea and the thimble caught their goose.

Two white-faced lurchers, not over-clean,
Urged the passers to "spot the Queen."
They flicked three cards that the world might choose,
They cried "All prizes. You cannot lose.
Come, pick the lady. Only a shilling."
One of their friends cried out, "I'm willing."
He "picked the lady" and took his pay,
And he cried, "It's giving money away."

Men came yelling "Cards of the races";
Men hawked matches and studs and laces;
Gipsy-women in green shawls dizened
Read girls' fortunes with eyes that glistened;
Negro ministrels on banjos strumming
Sang at the stiles to people coming.

Like glistening beetles clustered close,
The myriad motors parked in rows,

The bonnets flashed, and the brass did clink,
As the drivers poured their motors drink.
The March wind blew the smell of the crowd,
All men there seemed crying aloud,
But over the noise a louder roar
Broke, as the wave that bursts on shore,
Drowns the roar of the wave that comes,
So this roar rose on the lesser hums,
"I back the field.   I back the field."

Man who lives under sentence sealed,
Tragical man, who has but breath
For few brief years as he goes to death,
Tragical man by strange winds blown
To live in crowds ere he die alone,
Came in his jovial thousands massing,
To see Life moving and Beauty passing.

They sucked their fruit in the wooden tiers
And flung the skins at the passers' ears;
Drumming their heels on the planks below,
They sang of Dolly of Idaho.
Past, like a flash, the first race went.
The time drew by to the great event.

At a quarter to three the big bell pealed;
The horses trooped to the Saddling Field.
Covered in clothing, horse and mare
Pricked their ears at the people there;
Some showed devil, and some, composure,
As they trod their way to the great enclosure.

When the clock struck three and the men weighed out,
Charles Cothill shook, though his heart was stout.

The thought of his bets, so gaily laid,
Seemed a stone the more when he sat and weighed.

As he swung in the scales and nursed his saddle,
It seemed to him that his brains would addle;
For now that the plunger reached the brink,
The risk was more than he liked to think.

In ten more minutes his future life,
His hopes of home with his chosen wife,
Would all depend on a doubtful horse
In a crowded field over Compton Course.

He had backed Right Royal for all he owned.
At thought of his want of sense he groaned.
"All for a dream of the night," he thought.
He was right for weight at eleven naught.

Then Em's sweet face rose up in his brain,
He cursed his will that had dealt her pain:
To hurt sweet Emmy and lose her love
Was madman's folly by all above.
He saw too well as he crossed the yard
That his madman's plunge had borne her hard.
"To wring sweet Em like her drunken father,

I'd fall at the Pitch and end it rather.
Oh I hope, hope, hope, that her golden heart
Will give me a word before I start.
If I thought our love should have come to wreck,
I'd pull Right Royal and break my neck,
And Monkery's shoe might kick my brains out
That my own heart's blood might wash my stains out.

But even if Emmy, my sweet, forgive,
I'm a ruined man, so I need not live,

For I've backed my horse with my all, by Heaven,
To be first in a field of thirty-seven,
And good as he is, the dream's a lie."

He saw no hope, but to fall and die.

As he left the room for the Saddling Paddock
He looked as white as the flesh of haddock.
But Love, all seeing, though painted blind,
Makes wisdom live in a woman's mind:
His love knew well from her own heart's bleeding
The word of help that her man was needing;
And there she stood with her eyes most bright,
Ready to cheer her heart's delight.

She said, "My darling, I feel so proud
To see you followed by all the crowd;
And I shall be proud as I see you win.

Right Royal, Soyland and Peterkin
Are the three I pick, first, second, third.
And oh, now listen to what I heard.
Just now in the park Sir Norman Cooking
Said, 'Harding, how well Right Royal's looking.
They've brought him on in the ring, they say.'
John said, 'Sir Norman, to-day's his day.'
And Sir Norman said, 'If I had a monkey
I'd put it on yours, for he looks so spunky.'

So you see that the experts think as you.
Now, my own own own, may your dream come true,
As I know it will, as I know it must;
You have all my prayer and my love and trust.

Oh, one thing more that Sir Norman said,
'A lot of money has just been laid

On the mare Gavotte that no one knows.'
He said 'She's small, but, my word, she goes.
Since she bears no weight, if she only jumps,
She'll put these cracks to their ace of trumps.
But,' he said, 'she's slight for a course like this.'

That's all my gossip, so there it is.

Dear, reckon the words I spoke unspoken,
I failed in love and my heart is broken.
Now I go to my place to blush with pride
As the people talk of how well you ride;
I mean to shout like a bosun's mate
When I see you lead coming up the straight.
Now may all God's help be with you, dear."

"Well, bless you, Em, for your words of cheer.
And now is the woodcock near the gin.
Good-bye.
                    Now, Harding, we'd best begin."

At buckle and billet their fingers wrought,
Till the sheets were home and the bowlines taut.
As he knotted the reins and took his stand
The horse's soul came into his hand
And up from the mouth that held the steel
Came an innermost word, half thought, half feel,
"My day to-day, O master, O master;
None shall jump cleaner, none shall go faster,
Call till you kill me, for I'll obey,
It's my day to-day, it's my day to-day."

In a second more he had found his seat,
And the standers-by jumped clear of feet,
For the big dark bay all fire and fettle

Had his blood in a dance to show his mettle.
Charles soothed him down till his tricks were gone;
Then he leaned for a final word from John.

John Harding's face was alert and grim,
From under his hand he talked to him.
"It's none of my business, sir," he said,
"What you stand to win or the bets you've made,
But the rumour goes that you've backed your horse.

Now you need no telling of Compton Course.
It's a dangerous course at the best of times,
But on days like this some jumps are crimes;
With a field like this, nigh forty starting,
After one time round it'll need re-charting.

Now think it a hunt, the first time round;
Don't think too much about losing ground,
Lie out of your ground, for sure as trumps
There'll be people killed in the first three jumps.
The second time round, pipe hands for boarding,
You can see what's doing and act according.

Now your horse is a slug and a sulker too,
Your way with the horse I leave to you;
But, sir, you watch for these joker's tricks
And watch that devil on number six;
There's nothing he likes like playing it low,
What a horse mayn't like or a man mayn't know,
And what they love when they race a toff
Is to flurry his horse at taking off.
The ways of the crook are hard to learn.

Now watch that fence at the outer turn;
It looks so slight but it's highly like

That it's killed more men than the Dyers' Dyke.
It's down in a dip and you turn to take it,
And men in a bunch, just there, mistake it.
But well to the right, it's firmer ground,
And the quick way there is the long way round.
In Cannibal's year, in just this weather,
There were five came down at that fence together.
I called it murder, not riding races.
You've nothing to fear from the other places,
Your horse can jump.
                    Now I'll say no more.
They say you're on, as I said before.
It's none of my business, sir, but still
I would like to say that I hope you will.
Sir, I wish you luck. When we two next meet
I hope to hear how you had them beat."

Charles Cothill nodded with, "Thank you, John.
We'll try; and, oh, you're a thousand on."

He heard John's thanks, but knew at a glance
That John was sure that he stood no chance.

He turned Right Royal, he drew deep breath
With the thought "Now for it; a ride to death."
"Now come, my beauty, for dear Em's sake,
And if come you can't, may our necks both break."

And there to his front, with their riders stooping
For the final word, were the racers trooping.

Out at the gate to cheers and banter
They paced in pride to begin their canter.

Muscatel with the big white star,
The roan Red Ember, and Kubbadar,

Kubbadar with his teeth bared yellow
At the Dakkanese, his stable-fellow.
Then Forward-Ho, then a chestnut weed,
Skysail, slight, with a turn of speed.
The neat Gavotte under black and coral,
Then the Mutineer, Lord Leybourne's sorrel,
Natuna mincing, Syringa sidling,
Stormalong fighting to break his bridling,
Thunderbolt dancing with raw nerves quick,
Trying a savage at Bitter Dick.
The Ranger (winner three years before),
Now old, but ready for one try more;
Hadrian; Thankful; the stable-cronies,
Peterkinooks and Dear Adonis;
The flashing Rocket, with taking action;
Exception, backed by the Tencombe faction;
Old Sir Francis and young King Tony,
Culverin striding from great hips bony.

At this, he rode through the open gate
Into the course to try his fate.

He heard a roar from a moving crowd;
Right Royal kindled and cried aloud.
There was the course, stand, rail and pen,
Peopled with seventy thousand men;
Seventy thousand faces staring,
Carriages parked, a brass band blaring:
Over the stand the flags in billows
Bent their poles like the wands of willows.
All men there seemed trying to bawl,
Yet a few great voices topped them all:
"I back the field! I back the field!"

Right Royal trembled with pride and squealed.

Charles Cothill smiled with relief to find
This roaring crowd to his horse's mind.

He passed the stand where his lady stood,
His nerves were tense to the multitude;
His blood beat hard and his eyes grew dim
As he knew that some were cheering him.
Then, as he turned, at his pace's end
There came a roar as when floods descend.
All down the straight from the crowded stands
Came the yells of voices and clap of hands,
For with bright bay beauty that shone like flame
The favorite horse Sir Lopez came.

His beautiful hips and splendid shoulders
And power of stride moved all beholders,
Moved non-bettors to try to bet
On that favourite horse not beaten yet.
With glory of power and speed he strode
To a sea of cheering that moved and flowed
And followed and heaped and burst like storm
From the joy of men in the perfect form;
Cheers followed his path both sides the course.

Charles Cothill sighed when he saw that horse.

The cheering died, then a burst of clapping
Met Soyland's coming all bright from strapping,
A big dark brown who was booted thick
Lest one of the jumps should make him click.
He moved very big, he'd a head like a fiddle,
He seemed all ends without any middle,
But ill as he looked, that outcast racer
Was a rare good horse and a perfect chaser.
Then The Ghost came on, then Meringue, the bay,

Then proud Grey Glory, the dapple-grey;
The splendid grey brought a burst of cheers.
Then Cimmeroon, who had tried for years
And had thrice been placed and had once been fourth,
Came trying again the proverb's worth.

Then again, like a wave as it runs a pier,
On and on, unbroken, there came a cheer
As Monkery, black as a collier-barge,
Trod sideways, bickering, taking charge.
Cross-Molin, from the Blowbury, followed,
Lucky Shot skipped, Coranto wallowed,
Then Counter Vair, the declared-to-win,
Stable-fellow of Cross-Molin;
Culverin last, with Cannonade,
Formed rearguard to the grand parade.

And now, as they turned to go to post,
The Skysail calfishly barged The Ghost,
The Ghost lashed out with a bitter knock
On the tender muscle of Skysail's hock,
And Skysail's hope of that splendid hour
Was cut off short like a summer flower.
From the cantering crowd he limped apart
Back to the Paddock and did not start.

As they cantered down, Charles Cothill's mind
Was filled with joy that his horse went kind;
He showed no sulks, no sloth, no fear,
But leant on his rein and pricked his ear.
They lined themselves at the Post to start,
Charles took his place with a thumping heart.

Excitement running in waves took hold,
His teeth were chattered, his hands were cold,

His joy to be there was mixed with dread
To be left at post when they shot ahead.
The horses sparred as though drunk with wine,
They bickered and snatched at taking line.

Then a grey-haired man with a hawklike face
Read from a list each rider's place.
Sitting astride his pommely hack,
He ordered them up or sent them back;
He bade them heed that they jump their nags
Over every jump between the flags.
Here Kubbadar, who was pulling double,
Went sideways, kicking and raising trouble,
Monkery seconded, kicking and biting,
Thunderbolt followed by starting fighting.

The starter eyed them and gave the order
That the three wild horses keep the border,
With men to hold them to keep them quiet.
Boys from the stables stopped their riot.
Out of the line to the edge of the field,
The three wild biters and kickers wheeled;
Then the rest edged up and pawed and bickered,
Reached at their reins and snatched and snickered,
Flung white foam as they stamped their hate
Of passionate blood compelled to wait.

Then the starter shouted to Charles, "Good heaven,
This isn't a circus, you on Seven."
For Royal squirmed like a box of tricks
And Coranto's rider, the number Six,
Cursed at Charles for a green young fool
Who ought to be at a riding school.

After a minute of swerves and shoving,
A line like a half-moon started moving,

Then Rocket and Soyland leaped to stride,
To be pulled up short and wheeled to side.

Then the trickier riders started thrusting,
Judging the starter's mind too trusting;
But the starter said, "You know quite clearly
That isn't allowed; though you'd like it dearly."

Then Cannonade made a sideways bolt
That gave Exception an ugly jolt.
Then the line, reformed, broke all to pieces.
Then the line reforms, and the tumult ceases.
Each man sits tense though his racer dances;
In a slow, jerked walk the line advances.

And then in a flash, more felt than seen,
The flag shot down and the course showed green,
And the line surged forwards and all that glory
Of speed was sweeping to make a story.

One second before, Charles Cothill's mind
Had been filled with fear to be left behind,
But now with a rush, as when hounds leave cover,
The line broke up and his fear was over.
A glimmer of bay behind The Ghost
Showed Dear Adonis still there at post.
Out to the left, a joy to his backer,

Kubbadar led the field a cracker,
The thunder of horses, all fit and foaming,
Made the blood not care whether death were coming.
A glimmer of silks, blue, white, green, red,
Flashed into his eye and went ahead;
Then hoof-casts scattered, then rushing horses
Passed at his side with all their forces.

His blood leapt up but his mind said "No,
Steady, my darling, slow, go slow.
In the first time round this ride's a hunt."

The Turk's Grave Fence made a line in front.

Long years before, when the race began,
That first of the jumps had maimed a man;
His horse, the Turk, had been killed and buried
There in the ditch by horse-hoofs herried;
And over the poor Turk's bones at pace
Now, every year, there goes the race,
And many a man makes doctor's work
At the thorn-bound ditch that hides the Turk,
And every man as he rides that course
Thinks, there, of the Turk, that good old horse.

The thick thorn-fence stands five feet high,
With a ditch beyond unseen by eye,
Which a horse must guess from his urgent rider
Pressing him there to jump it wider.

And being so near both Stand and Post,
Out of all the jumps men haunt it most,
And there, with the crowd, and the undulled nerves,
The old horse balks and the young horse swerves,
And the good horse falls with the bad on top
And beautiful boldness comes to stop.

Charles saw the rush of the leading black,
And the forehands lift and the men sway back;
He steadied his horse, then with crash and crying
The top of the Turk's Grave Fence went flying.
Round in a flash, refusing danger,
Came the Lucky Shot right into Ranger;

Ranger swerving knocked Bitter Dick,
Who blundered at it and leaped too quick;
Then crash went blackthorn as Bitter Dick fell,
Meringue jumped on him and rolled as well.
As Charles got over he splashed the dirt
Of the poor Turk's grave on two men hurt.

Right Royal landed. With cheers and laughter
Some horses passed him and some came after;
A fine brown horse strode up beside him,
It was Thankful running with none to ride him;
Thankful's rider, dizzy and sick,
Lay in the mud by Bitter Dick.

In front, was the curving street of Course,
Barred black by the leaps unsmashed by horse.
A cloud blew by and the sun shone bright,
Showing the guard-rails gleaming white.
Little red flags, that gusts blew tense,
Streamed to the wind at each black fence.

And smiting the turf to clods that scattered
Was the rush of the race, the thing that mattered,
A tide of horses in fury flowing,
Beauty of speed in glory going,
Kubbadar pulling, romping first,
Like a big black fox that had made his burst.
And away and away and away they went,
A visible song of what life meant.
Living in houses, sleeping in bed,
Going to business, all seemed dead,
Dead as death to that rush in strife
Pulse for pulse with the heart of life.

"For to all," Charles thought, "when the blood beats high
Comes the glimpse of that which may not die;

When the world is stilled, when the wanting dwindles,
When the mind takes light and the spirit kindles,
One stands on a peak of this old earth."

Charles eyed his horses and sang with mirth.
What of this world that spins through space?
With red blood running he rode a race,
The beast's red spirit was one with his,
Emulous and in ecstasies;
Joy that from heart to wild heart passes
In the wild things going through the grasses;

In the hares in the corn, in shy gazelles
Running the sand where no man dwells;
In horses scared at the prairie spring;
In the dun deer noiseless, hurrying;
In fish in the dimness scarcely seen,
Save as shadows shooting in a shaking green;
In birds in the air, neck-straining, swift,
Wing touching wing while no wings shift,
Seen by none, but when stars appear
A reaper wandering home may hear
A sigh aloft where the stars are dim,
Then a great rush going over him:
This was his; it had linked him close
To the force by which the comet goes,
With the rein none sees, with the lash none feels,
But with fire-mane tossing and flashing heels.

The roar of the race-course died behind them,
In front were their Fates, they rode to find them,
With the wills of men, with the strengths of horses,
They dared the minute with all their forces.

PART II

Still pulling double, black Kubbadar led,
Pulling his rider half over his head;
Soyland's cream jacket was spotted with red,
Spotted with dirt from the rush of their tread.

Bright bay Sir Lopez, the loveliest there,
Galloped at ease as though taking the air,
Well in his compass with plenty to spare.
Gavotte and The Ghost and the brown Counter Vair,
Followed him close with Syringa the mare,
And the roan horse Red Ember who went like a hare,
And Forward-Ho bolting, though his rider did swear.

Keeping this order, they reached the next fence,
Which was living plashed blackthorn with gorse-toppings dense;
In the gloom of its darkness it loomed up immense.
And Forward-Ho's glory had conquered his sense
And he rushed it, not rising, and never went thence.

And down in the ditch where the gorse-spikes were scattered,
That bright chestnut's soul from his body was shattered,
And his rider shed tears on the dear head all spattered.

King Tony came down, but got up with a stumble,
His rider went sideways, but knew how to tumble,
And got up and remounted, though the pain made him humble,
And rode fifty yards and then stopped in a fumble.

With a rush and a crashing Right Royal went over
With the stride of a stalwart and the blood of a lover,
He landed on stubble now pushing with clover.

And just as he landed, the March sun shone bright
And the blue sky showed flamelike and the dun clouds turned
    white;
The little larks panted aloft their delight,
Trembling and singing as though one with the light.

And Charles, as he rode, felt the joy of their singing,
While over the clover the ho ses went stringing,
And up from Right Royal the message came winging,
"It is my day to-day, though the pace may be stinging,

Though the jumps be all danger and the going all clinging."
The white, square church-tower with its weather-cocks swinging,
Rose up on the right above grass and dark plough
Where the elm trees' black branches had bud on the bough.

Riderless Thankful strode on at his side,
His bright stirrup-irons flew up at each stride,
Being free, in this gallop, had filled him with pride.
Charles thought, "What would come, if he ran out or shied?
I wish from my heart that the brute would keep wide."
Coranto drew up on Right Royal's near quarter,
Beyond lay a hurdle and ditch full of water.
And now as they neared it, Right Royal took heed
Of the distance to go and the steps he would need;
He cocked to the effort with eyes bright as gleed,
Then Coranto's wide wallow shot past him at speed:
His rider's "Hup, hup, now!" called out quick and cheerly,
Sent him over in style, but Right Royal jumped early.

Just a second too soon, and from some feet too far,
Charles learned the mistake as he struck the top bar;
Then the water flashed skywards, the earth gave a jar,
And the man on Coranto looked back with "Aha!

That'll teach you, my son." Then with straining of leather,
Grey Glory and Monkery landed together.

For a second the stunning kept Charles from his pain,
Then his sense flooded back, making everything plain.
He was down on the mud, but he still held the rein;
Right Royal was heaving his haunch from the drain.
The field was ahead of him, going like rain,
And though the plough held them, they went like the wind
To the eyes of a man left so badly behind.

Charles climbed to his feet as Right Royal crawled out,
He said, "That's extinction beyond any doubt."
On the plough, on and on, went the rush of the rout.
Charles mounted and rode, for his courage was stout,
And he would not give in till the end of the bout,
But plastered with poachings he rode on forsaken:
He had lost thirty lengths and his horse had been shaken.

Across the wet ploughland he took a good pull,
With the thought that the cup of his sorrow was full,
For the speed of a stag and the strength of a bull
Could hardly recover the ground he had last.
Right Royal went dully, then snorted and tost,

Tost his head, with a whicker, went on, and went kind,
And the horse's great spirit touched Charles in the mind.
Though his bruise made him dizzy and tears made him blind,
He would try to the finish, and so they should find.
He was last, thirty lengths. Here he took in his sails,
For the field had come crash at the white post and rails.

Here Sir Francis ran out, scaring all who stood near,
Going crash through the rail like a runaway deer.
Then the riderless Thankful upset Mutineer,

Dakkanese, in refusing, wheeled round like a top
Into Culverin's shoulder which made them both stop.
They reeled from the shock, slithered sideways, and crashed,
Dakkanese on the guard-rail which gave, and then smashed.
As he rolled, the near shoes of the Culverin flashed
High in air for a moment, bright iron in strain:
Then he rose with no rider and tripped in his rein.

Right Royal came up as the Dakkanese rose
All trembling and cowed as though beaten with blows;
The Culverin stumbled with the reins in his toes;
On the far side the leap stood the Mutineer grazing
His man was a heap which some fellows were raising.
Right Royal strode on, through a second wet plough,
With the field far ahead (Kubbadar in the bow).
Charles thought, "Kubbadar's got away from him now.
Well, it's little to me, for they're so far ahead
That they'll never come back, though I ride myself dead."

Right Royal bored forward and leaned on his hand,
"Good boy," said his master. "He must understand.
You're the one friend I'll have when I've sold all my land.
God pity my Em as we come past the Stand,
Last of all, and all muddy; but now for Jim's Pitch."
Four feet of gorse fence, then a fifteen foot ditch.
And the fifteen foot ditch glittered bright to the brim
With the brook that ran through it where the grayling did swim;
In the shallows it sparkled, in the deeps it was dim,
When the race was first run it had nearly drowned Jim,
And now the bright irons of twenty-four horses
Were to flicker its ripples with knockings of gorses.

From far in the rear Charles could watch them take hold
Of their horses and push them across the light mould;

How their ears all cocked forward, how the drumming hoofs
    rolled!
Kubbadar, far ahead, flew across like a bird,
Then Soyland, bad second, with Muscatel third.
Then Sir Lopez, and Path Finder, striding alone,
Then the good horse, Red Ember, the flea-bitten roan.
Then the little Gavotte bearing less than ten stone.
Then a crowd of all colours with Peterkinooks
Going strong as a whale goes, head up and out flukes.

And then as Charles watched, as the shoulders went back,
The riderless Thankful swerved left off the track,
Crossing just to the front of the Cimmeroon black.
Ere the rider could see what his horse was about,
Cimmeroon swerved, like Thankful, and followed him out.
Across the great grass in the midst of the course
Cimmeroon ran a match race with the riderless horse,
Then the rider took charge, part by skill part by force;
He turned Cimmeroon to re-enter the race
Seven lengths behind Charles in the post of disgrace.

Beyond the next fence, at the top of a slope,
Charles saw his field fading and gave up all hope.
Yet he said, "Any error will knot me my rope.
I wish that some power would help me to see
What would give the best chance for Right Royal and me.
Shall I hurry downhill, to catch up when I can?
Being last is the devil for horse and for man,
For it makes the horse slack and it makes the man sick.
Well, I've got to decide and I've got to be quick.

I had better catch up, for if I should be last,
It would kill my poor Emmy to see me come past.
I cannot leave Emmy to suffer like that,
So I'll hurry downhill and then pull on the flat."

So he thought, so he settled, but then, as he stirred,
Right Royal's ears moved like a vicious man's word;
So he thought, "If I try it, the horse will refuse."
So he gave up the project and shook in his shoes.
Then he thought, "Since the horse will not stand interference,
I must even sit quiet and sink the appearance,
Since his nerves have been touched, it's as well we're alone."
He turned down the hill with his heart like a stone.

"But," he cried, "they'll come back, for they've gone such a
        bust
That they'll all soon be panting, in need to be nursed,
They will surely come back, but to wait till they do,
Lord, it's hell to the waiter, it cuts a man through."

Then into his mind came the Avalon case,
When a man, left at post, without hope of a place,
First had suffered in patience, then had wormed his way up,
Then had come with fine judgment, and just won the Cup.

Hoofs thundered behind him, the Cimmeroon caught him,
His man cursing Thankful and the sire who wrought him.
"Did you see that brown devil?" he cried as he passed;
"He carried me out, but I'll never be last.

Just the wrong side the water the brute gave a swerve,
And he carried me out, half across the course-curve.
Look, he's cut right across now, we'll meet him again.
Well, I hope someone knocks him and kicks out his brain.

Well, I'll never be last, though I can't win the Cup.
No sense lolling here, man, you'd better pull up."
Then he roused Cimmeroon, and was off like a swallow.

Charles watched, sick at heart, with a longing to follow.

"Better follow," he thought, "for he knows more than I,
Since he rode here before, and it's wiser to try:
Would my horse had but wings, would his feet would but lift;
Would we spun on this speedway as wind spins the drift.

There they go out of sight, over fence, to the Turn;
They are going still harder, they leave me astern.
They will never come back, I am lost past recall."
So he cried for a comfort and only gat gall.

In the glittering branches of the world without end,
Were the spirits, Em's Helper and Charles Cothill's Friend,
And the Force of Right Royal with a crinier of flame
There they breathed the bright glory till the summoning came.

From the Stand where Em watched, from the field where
      Charles rode,
From the mud where Right Royal in solitude strode,
Came the call of three spirits to the spirits that guard,
Crying, "Up now, and help him, for the danger bears hard."

There they looked, those immortals, from the boughs dropping
      balm,
But their powers were stirred not, and their grave brows were
      calm,
For they said, "He's despairing and the horse is still vext."
Charles cleared Channing's Blackthorn and strode to the next.

The next was the Turn in a bogland of rushes;
There the springs of still water were trampled to slushes;
The peewits lamented, flapping down, flagging far,
The riders dared deathwards each trusting his star.

The mud made them slither, the turn made them close,
The stirrup steels clinked as they thrust in their toes,

The brown horse Exception was struck as he rose,
Struck to earth by the Rocket, then kicked by the grey,
Then Thunderbolt smote him and rolled him astray.

The man on Exception, Bun Manor, fell clear
With Monkery's shoes half an inch from his ear,
A drench of wet mud from the hoofs struck his cheek,
But the race was gone from him before he could speak.

There Exception and Thunderbolt ended their race,
Their bright flanks all smeared with the mud of the place;
In the green fields of Tencombe and the grey downs of Churn
Their names had been glories till they fell at the Turn.

Em prayed in her place that her lover might know
Not to hurry Right Royal but let him go slow;
White-lipped from her praying, she sat, with shut eyes,
Begging help from her Helper, the deathless, the wise.

From the gold of his branches her Helper took heed,
He sent forth a thought to help Charles in his need.
As the white, gleaming gannet eyes fish in the sea,
So the thought sought a mortal to bring this to be.

By the side of Exception Bun Manor now stood
Sopping rags on a hock that was dripping bright blood.
He had known Charles of old and defeat made him kind,
The thought from the Helper came into his mind.

So he cried to Charles Cothill, "Go easy," he cried,
"Don't hurry; don't worry; sit still and keep wide.
They flowed like the Severn, they'll ebb like the tide.
They'll come back and you'll catch them." His voice died away.
In front lay the Dyke, deep as drowning, steel grey.

Charles felt his horse see it and stir at the sight.
Again his heart lifted to the dream of the night;
Once again in his heart's blood the horse seemed to say,
"I'll die or I'll do it.　It's my day to-day."

He saw the grey water in shade from its fence,
The rows of white faces all staring intense;
All the heads straining forward, all the shoulders packt dense.
Beyond, he saw Thankful, the riderless brown,
Snatching grass, dodging capture, with reins hanging down.

Then Thankful stopped eating and cocked up his head,
He eyed the swift horses that Kubbadar led,
His eye filled with fire at the roll of their tread;
Then he tore down the course with a flash of bright shoes,
As the race's bright herald on fire with news.

As Charles neared the water, the Rocket ran out
By jumping the railings and kicking a clout
Of rotten white woodwork to startle the trout.
When Charles cleared the water, the grass stretcht before
And the glory of going burned in to the core.

Far over his head with a whicker of wings
Came a wisp of five snipe from a field full of springs;
The gleam on their feathers went wavering past—
And then some men booed him for being the last.

But last though he was, all his blood was on fire
With the rush of the wind and the gleam of the mire,
And the leap of his heart to the skylarks in quire,
And the feel of his horse going onward, on, on,
Under sky with white banners and bright sun that shone.

Like a star in the night, like a spring in the waste,
The image of Emmy rose up as he raced,

Till his mind was made calm, and his spirit was braced.
For the prize was bright Emmy; his blood beat and beat
As her beauty made music in that thunder of feet.

The wind was whirled past him, it hummed in his ears,
Right Royal's excitement had banished his fears,
For his leap was like singing, his stride was like cheers,
All his blood was in glory, all his soul was blown bare,
They were one, blood and purpose, they strode through the air.

"What is life if I lose her, what is death if I win?
At the end of this living the new lives begin.
Whatever life may be, whatever death is,
I am spirit eternal, I am this, I am this!"

Girls waved, and men shouted, like flashes, like shots,
Out of pale blurs of faces whose features were dots;
Two fences with toppings were cleared without hitch,
Then they ran for Lost Lady's, a fence and dry ditch.

Here Monkery's rider, on seeing a chance,
Shot out beyond Soyland to lead the advance.
Then he steadied and summed up his field with a glance.
All crossed the Lost Lady's, that dry ditch of fear,
Then a roar broke about them, the racecourse was near.

Right and left were the swing-boats and merry-go-rounds,
Yellow varnish that wavered, machines making sounds,
Rifles cracking like cork-pops, fifes whining with steam,
"All hot," from a pieman; all blurred as in dream.

Then the motors, then cheering, then the brass of a band,
Then the white rails all crowded with a mob on each hand.
Then they swerved to the left over gorsebush and hurdle
And they rushed for the Water where a man's blood might
    curdle.

Charles entered the race-course and prayed in his mind
That love for the moment might make Emmy blind,
Not see him come past half a distance behind;
For an instant he thought, "I must shove on ahead,
For to pass her like this, Lord, I'd rather be dead."

Then, in crossing the hurdle the Stand arose plain,
All the flags, horns and cheers beat like blows on his brain,
And he thought, "Time to race when I come here again,
If I once lose my head, I'll be lost past appeal."
All the crowd flickered past like a film on a reel.

Like a ribbon, whirled past him, all painted with eyes.
All the real, as he rode, was the horse at his thighs,
And the thought "They'll come back, if I've luck, if I'm wise."
Some banners uncrumpled on the blue of the skies,
The cheers became frantic, the blur of men shook,
As Thankful and Kubbadar went at the brook.

Neck and neck, stride for stride, they increased as they neared
    it,
Though the danger gleamed greyly, they galloped to beard it;
And Kubbadar dwelt on his jump as he cleared it,
While Thankful went on with a half a length lead.
Charles thought, "Kubbadar, there, is going to seed."

Then Monkery took it, then Soyland, then two,
Muscatel and Sir Lopez, who leaped not but flew,
Like a pair of June swallows going over the dew,
Like a flight of bright fishes from a field of seas blue,
Like a wisp of snipe wavering in the dusk out of view.
Then Red Ember, Path Finder, Gavotte and Coranto,
Then The Ghost going level by Syringa a-taunto,

Then Peterkinooks, then the Cimmeroon black,
Who had gone to his horses, not let them come back;

Then Stormalong rousing, then the Blowbury crack,
Counter Vair, going grandly beside Cross-Molin,
All charged the bright brook and Coranto went in.

Natuna, Grey Glory and Hadrian followed,
Flying clear of the water where Coranto now wallowed;
Cannonade leaped so big that the lookers-on holloed.
Ere the splash from Coranto was bright on the grass,
The face of the water had seen them all pass.
But Coranto half scrambled, then slipped on his side,
Then churned in the mud till the brook was all dyed;
As Charles reached the water Coranto's man cried,
"Put him at it like blazes and give him a switch;
Jump big, man, for God's sake, I'm down in the ditch."

Right Royal went at it and streamed like a comet,
And the next thing Charles knew, he was twenty yards from it;
And he thought about Em as he rushed past her place,
With a prayer for God's peace on her beautiful face.

Then he tried to keep steady. "O steady," he said,
"I'm riding with judgment, not leading a raid,
And I'm getting excited, and there's Cannonade.
What's the matter?" he shouted, as Royal swept past.
"Sprained!" shouted the man, "Over-jumped, at the last."

"Rough luck," shouted Charles. Then the crowd dropped away,
Then the sun shone behind him, the bright turned to grey;
They were round, the first time, they were streaming away
For the second time round. There the starting-post shone.
Then they swung round the curve and went galloping on.

All the noise died behind, Fate was waiting in front,
Now the racing began, they had done with the hunt.

With the sunlight behind him Charles saw how they went;
No nearer, but further, and only one spent.

Only Kubbadar dwelling, the rest going strong,
Taking jump after jump as a bird takes a song,
Their thirty lengths' lead seemed a weary way long,
It seemed to grow longer, it seemed to increase:
"This is bitter," he said.   "May it be for my peace.

My dream was a glimpse of the world beyond sense,
All beauty and wisdom are messages thence.
There the difference of bodies and the strain of control
Are removed; beast with man speaks, and spirit with soul.

My vision was wisdom, or the World as it Is.
Fate rules us, not Wisdom, whose ways are not his,
Fate, weaponed with all things, has willed that I fall;
So be it, Fate orders, and we go to the wall.

Go down to the beaten, who have come to the truth
That is deeper than sorrow and stronger than youth,
That is God, the foundation, who sees and is just
To the beauty within us who are nothing but dust.

Yet, Royal, my comrade, before Fate decides,
His hand stays, uncertain, like the sea between tides,
Then a man has a moment, if he strike not too late,
When his soul shakes the world-soul, and can even change Fate.

So you and I, Royal, before we give in
Will spend blood and soul in our effort to win,
And if all be proved vain when our effort is sped,
May the hoofs of our conquerors trample us dead."

Then the soul of Right Royal thrilled up through each hand,
"We are one, for this gallop; we both understand.

If my lungs give me breathing, if my loins stand the strain,
You may lash me to strips and it shan't be in vain.

For to-day, in this hour, my Power will come
From my Past to my Present (and a Spirit gives some).
We have gone many gallops, we two, in the past,
When I go with my Power you will know me at last.

You remember the morning when the red leaf hung still,
When they found in the beech-clump on Lollingdon Hill,
When we led past the Sheep Fold and along the Fair Mile?
When I go with my Power, that will not seem worth while.

Then the day in the valley when we found in the wood,
When we led all the gallop to the river in flood,
And the sun burst out shining as the fox took the stream,
When I go with my Power, that will all seem a dream.

Then the day on the Downland when we went like the light
From the spring by Hurst Compton till the Clump was in sight,
Till we killed by The Romans, where Blowbury is,
All the best of that gallop shall be nothing to this.

If I failed in the past with my Power away,
I was only my shadow, it was not my day,
So I sulked like my sire, or shrank, like my dam;
Now I come to my Power you will know what I am.

I've the strength, you've the brain, we are running as one
And nothing on earth can be lost till it's won.
If I live to the end, naught shall put you to shame."
So he thrilled, going flame-like, with a crinier of flame.

"Yet," he thrilled, "It may be, that before the end come
Death will touch me, the Changer, and carry me home.

For we know not, O master, when our life shall have rest,
But the Life is near change that has uttered its best.
If we grow like the grasses, we fall like the flower,
And I know, I touch Death when I come to my Power."

Now over the course flew invisible birds,
All the Wants of the Watchers, all the thoughts and winged
    words,
Swift as floatings of fire from a bonfire's crest
When they burn leaves on Kimble and the fire streams west,

Bright an instant, then dying, but renewed and renewed,
So the thoughts chased the racers like hounds that pursued,
Bringing cheer to their darlings, bringing curse to their foes,
Searching into men's spirits till their Powers arose.

Red and rigid the Powers of the riding men were,
And as sea birds on Ailsa, in the nesting time there,
Rise like leaves in a whirlwind and float like leaves blown,
So the wants chased the riders and fought for their own.

Unseen by the riders, from the myriad tense brains
Came the living thoughts flying to clutch at men's reins,
Clearing paths for their darlings by running in cry
At the heads of their rivals till the darlings gat by

As in football, when forwards heave all in a pack,
With their arms round each other and their heels heeling back,
And their bodies all straining, as they heave, and men fall,
And the halves hover hawklike to pounce on the ball,

And the runners poise ready, while the mass of hot men
Heaves and slips, like rough bullocks making play in a pen,
And the crowd sees the heaving, and is still, till it break,
So the riders endeavoured as they strained for the stake.

They skimmed through the grassland, they came to the plough,
The wind rushed behind them like the waves from a prow,
The clods rose behind them with speckles of gold
From the iron-crusht coltsfoot flung up from the mould.

All green was the plough with the thrusts of young corn,
Pools gleamed in the ruts that the cartwheels had worn,
And Kubbadar's man wished he had not been born.
Natuna was weary and dwelt on her stride,
Grey Glory's grey tail rolled about, side to side.

Then swish, came a shower, from a driving grey cloud
Though the blue sky shone brightly and the larks sang aloud.
As the squall of rain pelted, the coloured caps bowed,
With Thankful still leading and Monkery close,
The hoofs smacked the clayland, the flying clods rose.

They slowed on the clayland, the rain pelted by,
The end of a rainbow gleamed out in the sky;
Natuna dropped back till Charles heard her complain,
Grey Glory's forequarters seemed hung on his rein,
Cimmeroon clearly was feeling the strain.
But the little Gavotte skimmed the clay like a witch,
Charles saw her coquet as she went at Jim's Pitch.

They went at Jim's Pitch, through the deeply dug gaps
Where the hoofs of great horses had kicked off the scraps,
And there at the water they met with mishaps,
For Natuna stopped dead and Grey Glory went in
And a cannon on landing upset Cross-Molin.

As swallows bound northward when apple-bloom blows,
See laggards drop spent from their flight as it goes,
Yet can pause not in Heaven as they scythe the thin air
But go on to the house-eaves and the nests clinging bare,

So Charles flashed beyond them, those three men the less
Who had gone to get glory and met with distress.

He rode to the rise-top, and saw, down the slope,
The race far ahead at a steady strong lope
Going over the grassland, too well for his peace,
They were steady as oxen and strong as wild geese.

As a man by a cornfield on a windy wild day
Sees the corn bow in shadows ever hurrying away,
And wonders, in watching, when the light with bright feet
Will harry those shadows from the ears of the wheat,
So Charles, as he watched, wondered when the bright face
Of the finish would blaze on that smouldering race.

On the last of the grass, ere the going was dead,
Counter Vair's man shot out with his horse by the head,
Like a partridge put up from the stubble he sped,
He dropped Kubbadar and he flew by Red Ember
Up to Monkery's girth like a leaf in November.

Then Stormalong followed, and went to the front,
And just as the find puts a flame to a hunt,
So the rush of those horses put flame to the race.
Charles saw them all shaken to quickening pace.
And Monkery moved, not to let them go by,
And the steadiest rider made ready to fly;
Well into the wet land they leaped from the dry,
They scattered the rain-pools that mirrored the sky,
They crushed down the rushes that pushed from the plough.
And Charles longed to follow, but muttered "Not now."

"Not now," so he thought, "Yet if not" (he said) "when
Shall I come to those horses and scupper their men?
Will they never come back? Shall I never get up?"
So he drank bitter gall from a very cold cup.

But he nursed his horse gently and prayed for the best,
And he caught Cimmeroon, who was sadly distrest,
And he passed Cimmeroon, with the thought that the black
Was as nearly dead beat as the man on his back.
Then he gained on his field who were galled by the Churn,
The plough searched them out as they came to the Turn.
But Gavotte, black and coral, went strong as a spate
Charles thought "She's a flier and she carries no weight."

And now, beyond question the field began tailing,
For all had been tested and many were ailing,
The riders were weary, the horses were failing,
The blur of bright colours rolled over the railing.
With the grunts of urged horses, and the oaths of hot men,
"Gerr on, you," "Come on, now," agen and agen;
They spattered the mud on the willow tree's bole
And they charged at the danger; and the danger took toll.

For Monkery landed, but dwelt on the fence
So that Counter Vair passed him in galloping thence.
Then Stormalong blundered, then bright Muscatel
Slipped badly on landing and stumbled and fell,

Then rose in the morrish, with his man on his neck
Like a nearly dead sailor afloat on a wreck,
With his whip in the mud and his stirrups both gone,
Yet he kept in the saddle and made him go on.

As Charles leaped the Turn, all the field was tailed out
Like petals of roses that wind blows about,
Like petals of colour blown back and brought near,
Like poppies in wind-flaws when corn is in ear,
Fate held them or sped them, the race was beginning.
Charles said, "I must ride, or I've no chance of winning,"

So gently he quickened, yet making no call;
Right Royal replied as though knowing it all,
He passed Kubbadar who was ready to fall,
Then he strode up to Hadrian, up to his girth,
They eyed the Dyke's glitter and picked out a berth.
Now the race reached the water and over it flew
In a sweep of great muscle strained taut and guyed true.
There Muscatel floundered and came to a halt,
Muscatel, the bay chaser without any fault.

Right Royal's head lifted, Right Royal took charge,
On the left near the railings, ears cocked, going large,
Leaving Hadrian behind as a yacht leaves a barge.
Though Hadrian's rider called something unheard,
He was past him at speed like the albatross bird,
Running up to Path Finder, they leaped, side by side,
And the foam from Path Finder flecked white on his hide.
And on landing, he lifted, while Path Finder dwelt,
And his noble eye brightened from the glory he felt,
And the mud flung behind him flicked Path Finder's chest,
As he left him behind and went on to the rest.

Charles cast a glance back, but he could not divine
Why the man on Path Finder should make him a sign,
Nor why Hadrian's rider should shout, and then point,
With his head nodded forward and a jerked elbow joint.

But he looked as he pointed, both forward and down,
And he saw that Right Royal was smeared like a clown,
Smeared red and bespattered with flecks of bright blood,
From a blood-vessel burst, as he well understood.

And just as he saw it, Right Royal went strange
As one whom Death's finger has touched to a change;

He went with a stagger that sickened the soul,
As a force stricken feeble and out of control.

Charles thought, "He is dying, and this is the end,
I am losing my Emmy and killing my friend;
He was hurt when we fell, as I thought at the first,
And I've forced him three miles with a blood-vessel burst.

And his game heart went on." Here a rush close behind
Made him cast a glance back with despair in his mind.
It was Cimmeroon rushing, his lips twitcht apart,
His eyes rolled back sightless, and death in his heart.
He reached to Right Royal, then fell, and was dead,
Nevermore to stretch reins with his beautiful head.

A gush of bright blood filled his mouth as he sank,
And he reached out his hoofs to the heave of his flank,
And Charles, leaning forward, made certain, and cried,
"This is Cimmeroon's blood, blown in passing beside,
And Roy's going strangely was just that he felt
Death coming behind him, or blood that he smelt."

So Charles's heart lightened and Royal went steady
As a water bound seaward set free from an eddy,
As a water sucked downward to leap at a weir
Sucked swifter and swifter till it shoot like a spear.

There, a mile on ahead, was the Stand like a cliff,
Grey wood, packed with faces, under banners blown stiff,
Where, in two minutes more, they would cheer for him—if—
If he came to those horses still twelve lengths ahead.
"O Royal, you do it, or kill me!" he said.

They went at the hurdle as though it weren't there,
White splinters of hurdle flew up in the air,

And down, like a rabbit, went Syringa the mare;
Her man somersaulted right under Gavotte,
And Syringa went on but her rider did not.

But the little Gavotte tucked her feet away clear,
Just an inch to one side of the fallen man's ear,
With a flash of horse wisdom as she went on the wing
Not to tread on man's body, that marvellous thing.

As in mill-streams in summer the dark water drifts
Petals mown in the hayfield skimmed over by swifts,
Petals blue from the speedwell or sweet from the lime,
And the fish rise to test them, as they float, for a time,
Yet they all loiter sluicewards and are whirled, and then
    drowned,
So the race swept the horses till they glimmered the ground.

Charles looked at those horses, and speedily guesst
That the roan horse, Red Ember, was one of the best;
He was level and easy, not turning a hair,
But with power all ready when his rider should care,
And he leaped like a lover and his coat still did shine.
Charles thought, "He's a wonder, and he's twelve lengths from
    mine."

There were others still in it, according to looks:—
Sir Lopez, and Soyland, and Peterkinooks,
Counter Vair and Gavotte, all with plenty to spend;
Then Monkery worn, and The Ghost at his end.
But the roan horse, Red Ember, seemed playing a game.
Charles thought, "He's the winner; he can run us all tame."
The wind brought a tune and a faint noise of cheers,
Right Royal coquetted and cocked up his ears.

Charles saw his horse gaining; the going increased;
His touch on the mouth felt the soul of the beast,

And the heave of each muscle and the look of his eye
Said, "I'll come to those horses, and pass them, or die."

Like a thing in a dream the grey buildings drew nearer,
The babble rose louder and the organ's whine clearer,
The hurdle came closer, he rushed through its top
Like a comet in heaven that nothing can stop.

Then they strode the green grass for the Lost Lady's grave,
And Charles felt Right Royal rise up like a wave,
Like a wave far to seaward that lifts in a line
And advances to shoreward in a slipping incline,

And climbs, and comes toppling, and advances in glory,
Mounting inwards, marching onwards, with his shoulders all
    hoary,
Sweeping shorewards with a shouting to burst on the sand,
So Right Royal sent meaning through the rein in each hand.

Charles felt like a captain whose ship has long chased
Some ship better handled, better manned, better placed,
And has all day beheld her, that ship of his dream,
Bowing swanlike beyond him up a blue hill of gleam,

Yet, at dark, the wind rising makes his rival strike sail
While his own ship crowds canvas and comes within hail;
Till he see her, his rival, snouting into the grey,
Like a sea-rock in winter that stands and breaks spray,
And by lamplight goes past her in a roaring of song
Shouting, "Let fall your royals: stretch the halliards along!"

Now The Ghost dropped behind him, now his horses drew close.
Charles watched them, in praying, while his hopes rose and rose,
"O God, give me patience, give me luck, give me skill,
For he's going so grandly I think that he will."

They went at Lost Lady's like Severn at flood,
With an urging of horses and a squelching of mud;
By the hot flanks of horses the toppings were bruised,
And Syringa the manless swerved right and refused.

Swerved right on a sudden, as none could expect,
Straight into Right Royal, who slithered and pecked,
Though Charles held him up and got safely across,
He was round his nag's neck within touch of a toss

He gat to his saddle, he never knew how;
What hope he had had was knocked out of him now,
But his courage came back as his terror declined,
He spoke to Right Royal and made up his mind.
He judged the lengths lost and the chance that remained,
And he followed his field, and he gained, and he gained.

He watched them, those horses, so splendid, so swift,
Whirled down the green roadway like leaves in the lift:
Now he measured their mettle, and said with a moan,
"They can beat me, Lord help me, though they give me a stone.
Red Ember's a wonder, and Soyland's the same,
And Gavotte there's a beauty, and she goes like a flame;
But Peterkinooks, that I used to despise,
Is the horse that must win if his looks are not lies."

There bright colours flitted as at dusk in Brazil
Bright birds reach the tree-tops when the land wind falls still,
When the sky is all scarlet on the tops of the treen
Comes a whirl of birds flying, blue and orange and green.

As a whirl of notes running in a fugue that men play,
And the thundering follows as the pipe flits away,
And the laughter comes after and the hautboys begin,
So they ran at the hurdle and scattered the whin.

As they leaped to the race-course the sun burst from cloud
And like tumult in dream came the roar of the crowd.

For to right and to left, now, were crowded men yelling,
And a great cry boomed backward like muffled bells knelling,
And a surge of men running seemed to follow the race,
The horses all trembled and quickened their pace.

As the porpoise, grown weary of his rush through the dim
Of the unlitten silence where the swiftnesses swim,
Learns at sudden the tumult of a clipper bound home
And exults with this playmate and leaps in her foam,

Or as nightingales coming into England in May,
Coming songless at sunset, being worn with the way,
Settle spent in the twilight, drooping head under wing,
Yet are glad when the dark comes, while at moonrise they sing;

Or as fire on a hillside, by happy boys kindled,
That has burnt black a heath-tuft, scorcht a bramble, and
    dwindled,
Blown by wind yet arises in a wave of flogged flame,
So the souls of those horses to the testing time came.

Now they closed on their leaders, and the running increased,
They rushed down the arc curving round to the east;
All the air rang with roaring, all the peopled loud stands
Roared aloud from tense faces, shook with hats and waved
    hands.

So they cleared the green gorse-bush by bursting it through,
There was no time for thinking, there was scarce time to do.
Charles gritted his spirit as he charged through the gorse:
"You must just grin and suffer: sit still on your horse."

There in front was a hurdle and the Distance Post white,
And the long, green, broad Straight washed with wind and blown
    bright;
Now the roaring had screaming, bringing names to their ears:
"Come, Soyland!" "Sir Lopez!" Then catcalls; then cheers.

"Sir Lopez! Sir Lopez!" then the jigging brass laughter
From the yellow tost swing-boats swooping rafter to rafter.
Then the blare of all organs, then the roar of all throats,
And they shot past the side shows, the horses and boats.

Now the Wants of the Watchers whirled into the race
Like flames in their fury, like men in the face,
Mad-red from the Wanting that made them alive,
They fought with those horses or helped them to strive.

Like leaves blown on Hudson when maples turn gold,
They whirled in their colour, they clutched to catch hold,
They sang to the riders, they smote at their hearts
Like flakes of live fire, like castings of darts.

As a snow in Wisconsin when the darkness comes down,
Running white on the prairie, making all the air brown,
Blinding men with the hurry of its millions of feet,
So the Wants pelted on them, so they blinded and beat.

And like spirits calm shining upon horses of flame,
Came the Friends of those riders to shield them from shame,
White as fire white-burning, rushing each by his friend,
Singing songs of the glory of the world without end;

And as men in Wisconsin driving cars in the snow
Butt against its impulsion and face to the blow,
Tossing snow from their bonnets as a ship tosses foam,
So the Friends tossed the Wantings as they brought their friends
    home.

Now they charged the last hurdle that led to the Straight,
Charles longing to ride, though his spirit said "Wait."
He came to his horses as they came to the leap,
Eight hard-driven horses, eight men breathing deep.

On the left, as he leaped it, a flashing of brown
Kicking white on the grass, showed that Thankful was down;
Then a glance right and left showed, that barring all flukes,
It was Soyland's, Sir Lopez', or Peterkinooks'.

For Stormalong blundered and dwelt as he landed,
Counter Vair's man was beaten and Monkery stranded.
As he reached to Red Ember the man on the red
Cried, "Lord, Charlie Cothill, I thought you were dead!"

He passed the Red Ember, he came to the flank
Of Peterkinooks, whom he reached and then sank.
There were only two others, going level alone,
First the spotted cream jacket, then the blue, white and roan.

Up the street of green race-course they strained for the prize,
While the stands blurred with waving and the air shook with
    cries:
"Now, Sir Lopez!" "Come, Soyland!" "Now, Sir Lopez!
    Now, now!"
Then Charles judged his second, but he could not tell how.

But a glory of sureness leaped from horse into man,
And the man said, "Now, beauty," and the horse said, "I can."
And the long weary Royal made an effort the more,
Though his heart thumped like drum-beats as he went to the
    fore.

Neck and neck went Sir Lopez and Soyland together,
Soyland first, a short head, with his neck all in lather;

Both were ridden their hardest, both were doing their best,
Right Royal reached Soyland and came to his chest.

There Soyland's man saw him with the heel of his eye,
A horse with an effort that could beat him or tie;
Then he glanced at Sir Lopez, and he bit through his lip,
And he drove in his spurs and he took up his whip.

There he lashed the game Soyland who had given his all,
And he gave three strides more, and then failed at the call,
And he dropped behind Royal like a leaf in a tide:
Then Sir Lopez and Royal ran on side by side.

There they looked at each other, and they rode, and were grim;
Charles thought, "That's Sir Lopez. I shall never beat him."
All the yells for Sir Lopez seemed to darken the air,
They were rushing past Emmy and the White Post was there.

He drew to Sir Lopez; but Sir Lopez drew clear;
Right Royal clung to him and crept to his ear.
Then the man on Sir Lopez judged the moment had come
For the last ounce of effort that would bring his horse home.

So he picked up his whip for three swift slashing blows,
And Sir Lopez drew clear, but Right Royal stuck close.
Charles sat still as stone, for he dared not to stir—
There was that in Right Royal that needed no spur.

In the trembling of an instant power leaped up within,
Royal's pride of high spirit not to let the bay win.
Up he went, past his withers, past his neck, to his head,
With Sir Lopez' man lashing, Charles still, seeing red.

So they rushed for one second, then Sir Lopez shot out:
Charles thought, "There, he's done me, without any doubt.

O come now, Right Royal!"
And Sir Lopez changed feet
And his ears went back level; Sir Lopez was beat.

Right Royal went past him, half an inch, half a head,
Half a neck, he was leading, for an instant he led;
Then a hooped black and coral flew up like a shot,
With a lightning-like effort from little Gavotte.

The little bright mare, made of nerves and steel springs,
Shot level beside him, shot ahead as with wings.
Charles felt his horse quicken, felt the desperate beat
Of the blood in his body from his knees to his feet.

Three terrible strides brought him up to the mare,
Then they rushed to wild shouting through a whirl of blown air;
Then Gavotte died to nothing; Soyland came once again
Till his muzzle just reached to the knot on his rein.

Then a whirl of urged horses thundered up, whipped and blown,
Soyland, Peterkinooks, and Red Ember the roan.
For an instant they challenged, then they drooped and were
done;
Then the White Post shot backwards, Right Royal had won.

Won a half length from Soyland, Red Ember close third;
Fourth, Peterkinooks; fifth, Gavotte harshly spurred;
Sixth, Sir Lopez, whose rider said "Just at the Straight
He swerved at the hurdle and twisted a plate."

Then the numbers went up; then John Harding appeared
To lead in the Winner while the bookmakers cheered.
Then the riders weighed-in, and the meeting was over,
And bright Emmy Crowthorne could go with her lover.

For the bets on Right Royal which Cothill had made
The taker defaulted, they never were paid;
The taker went West, whence he sent Charles's bride
Silver bit-cups and beadwork on antelope hide.

Charles married his lady, but he rode no more races;
He lives on the Downland on the blown grassy places,
Where he and Right Royal can canter for hours
On the flock bitten turf full of tiny blue flowers.

There the Roman pitcht camp, there the Saxon kept sheep,
There he lives out this Living that no man can keep,
That is manful but a moment before it must pass,
Like the stars sweeping westward, like the wind on the grass.

KING COLE

King Cole was King before the troubles came,
The land was happy while he held the helm,
The valley-land from Condicote to Thame,
Watered by Thames and green with many an elm.
For many a year he governed well his realm,
So well-beloved, that, when at last he died,
It was bereavement to the countryside.

So good, so well-beloved, had he been
In life, that when he reached the judging-place
(There where the scales are even, the sword keen),
The Acquitting Judges granted him a grace,
Aught he might choose, red, black, from king to ace,
Beneath the bright arch of the heaven's span;
He chose, to wander earth, the friend of man.

So, since that time, he wanders shore and shire,
An old, poor, wandering man, with glittering eyes
Helping distressful folk to their desire
By power of spirit that within him lies.
Gentle he is, and quiet, and most wise,
He wears a ragged grey, he sings sweet words,
And where he walks there flutter little birds.

And when the planets glow as dusk begins
He pipes a wooden flute to music old.
Men hear him on the downs, in lonely inns,
In valley woods, or up the Chiltern wold;
His piping feeds the starved and warms the cold,
It gives the beaten courage; to the lost
It brings back faith, that lodestar of the ghost.

And most he haunts the beech-tree-pasturing chalk,
The Downs and Chilterns with the Thames between.
There still the Berkshire shepherds see him walk,
Searching the unhelped woe with instinct keen,
His old hat stuck with never-withering green,
His flute in poke, and little singings sweet
Coming from birds that flutter at his feet.

Not long ago a circus wandered there,
Where good King Cole most haunts the public way,
Coming from Reading for St. Giles's Fair
Through rain unceasing since Augustine's Day;
The horses spent, the waggons splashed with clay,
The men with heads bowed to the wester roaring,
Heaving the van-wheels up the hill at Goring.

Wearily plodding up the hill they went,
Broken by bitter weather and the luck,
Six vans, and one long waggon with the tent,
And piebald horses following in the muck,
Dragging their tired hooves out with a suck,
And heaving on, like some defeated tribe
Bound for Despair with Death upon their kibe.

All through the morn the circus floundered thus,
The nooning found them at the Crossing Roads,
Stopped by an axle splitting in its truss.
The horses drooped and stared before their loads.
Dark with the wet they were, and cold as toads.
The men were busy with the foundered van,
The showman stood apart, a beaten man.

He did not heed the dripping of the rain,
Nor the wood's roaring, nor the blotted hill,
He stood apart and bit upon his pain,

Biting the bitter meal with bitter will.
Focussed upon himself, he stood, stock still,
Staring unseeing, while his mind repeated,
"This is the end; I'm ruined; I'm defeated."

From time to time a haggard woman's face
Peered at him from a van, and then withdrew;
Seeds from the hayrack blew about the place,
The smoke out of the waggon chimneys blew,
From wicker creel the skinny cockerel crew.
The men who set the floundered axle straight
Glanced at their chief, and each man nudged his mate.

And one, the second clown, a snub-nosed youth,
Fair-haired, with broken teeth, discolored black,
Muttered, "He looks a treat, and that's the truth.
I've had enough: I've given him the sack."
He took his wrench, arose, and stretched his back,
Swore at a piebald pony trying to bite,
And rolled a cigarette and begged a light.

Within, the second's wife, who leaped the hoops,
Nursed sour twins, her son and jealousy,
Thinking of love, in luckier, happier troupes
Known on the roads in summers now gone by
Before her husband had a roving eye,
Before the rat-eyed baggage with red hair
Came to do tight rope and make trouble there.

Beside the vans, the clown, old Circus John,
Growled to the juggler as he sucked his briar,
"How all the marrow of a show was gone
Since women came, to sing and walk the wire,
Killing the clown his act for half his hire,

Killing the circus trade: because," said he,
"Horses and us are what men want to see."

The juggler was a young man shaven-clean,
Even in the mud his dainty way he had,
Red-cheeked, with eyes like boxer's, quick and keen,
A jockey-looking youth with legs besprad,
Humming in baritone a ditty sad,
And tapping on his teeth his finger-nails,
The while the clown suckt pipe and spat his tales.

Molly, the singer, watched him wearily
With big black eyes that love had brimmed with tears,
Her mop of short cut hair was blown awry,
Her firm mouth shewed her wiser than her years.
She stroked a piebald horse and pulled his ears,
And kissed his muzzle, while her eyes betrayed
This, that she loved the juggler, not the jade.

And growling in a group the music stood
Sucking short pipes, their backs against the rain,
Plotting rebellion in a bitter mood,
"A shilling more, or never play again."
Their old great coats were foul with many a stain,
Weather and living rough had stamped their faces,
They were cast clerks, old sailors, old hard cases.

Within the cowboy's van the rat-eyed wife,
Her reddish hair in papers twisted close,
Turned wet potatoes round against the knife,
And in a bucket dropped the peelèd Oes.
Her little girl was howling from her blows,
The cowboy smoked and with a spanner whackt
The metal target of his shooting act.

And in another van more children cried
From being beaten or for being chid
By fathers cross or mothers haggard-eyed,
Made savage by the fortunes that betide.
The rain dripped from the waggons: the drops glid
Along the pony's flanks; the thick boots stamped
The running muck for warmth, and hope was damped.

Yet all of that small troupe in misery stuck,
Were there by virtue of their nature's choosing
To be themselves and take the season's luck,
Counting the being artists worth the bruising.
To be themselves, as artists, even if losing
Wealth, comfort, health, in doing as they chose,
Alone of all life's ways brought peace to those.

So there below the forlorn woods, they grumbled,
Stamping for warmth and shaking off the rain.
Under the foundered van the tinkers fumbled,
Fishing the splitted truss with wedge and chain.
Soon, all was done, the van could go again,
Men cracked their whips, the horses' shoulders forged
Up to the collar while the mud disgorged.

So with a jangling of their chains they went,
Lean horses, swaying vans and creaking wheels,
Bright raindrops tilting off the van roof pent
And reedy cockerels crying in the creels,
Smoke driving down, men's shouts and children's squeals,
Whips cracking, and the hayrack sheddings blowing;
The Showman stood aside to watch them going.

What with the rain and misery making mad,
The Showman never saw a stranger come

Till there he stood, a stranger roughly clad
In ragged grey of woolen spun at home.
Green sprigs were in his hat, and other some
Stuck in his coat; he bore a wooden flute,
And redbreasts hopped and carolled at his foot.

It was King Cole, who smiled and spoke to him.

KING COLE:	The mend will hold until you reach a wright. Where do you play?
THE SHOWMAN:	In Wallingford to-night.
KING COLE:	There are great doings there.
THE SHOWMAN:	I know of none.
KING COLE:	The Prince will lay the Hall's foundation stone This afternoon: he and the Queen are there.
THE SHOWMAN:	Lord, keep this showman patient, lest he swear.
KING COLE:	Why should you swear? Be glad; your town is filled.
THE SHOWMAN:	What use are crowds to me with business killed?
KING COLE:	I see no cause for business to be crosst.
THE SHOWMAN:	Counter-attractions, man, at public cost. Fireworks, dancing, bonfires, soldiers, speeches. In all my tour along the river's reaches I've had ill-luck: I've clashed with public feasts. At Wycombe fair, we met performing beasts, At Henley, waxworks, and at Maidenhead The Psyche woman talking with the dead. At Bray, we met the rain, at Reading, flood, At Pangbourne, politics, at Goring, mud. Now here, at Wallingford, the Royal Pair. Counter-attraction killing everywhere, Killing a circus dead: God give me peace;

If this be living, death will be release.
By God, it brims the cup; it fills the can.
What trade are you?

KING COLE: I am a wandering man.

THE SHOWMAN: You mean, a tramp who flutes for bread and pence?

KING COLE: I come, and flute, and then I wander thence.

THE SHOWMAN: Quicksilver Tom, who couldn't keep his place.

KING COLE: My race being run, I love to watch the race.

THE SHOWMAN: You ought to seek your rest.

KING COLE: My rest is this,
The world of men, wherever trouble is.

THE SHOWMAN: If trouble rests you, God! your life is rest.

KING COLE: Even the sun keeps moving, east to west.

THE SHOWMAN: Little he gets by moving; less than I.

KING COLE: He sees the great green world go floating by.

THE SHOWMAN: A sorry sight to see, when all is said. Why don't you set to work?

KING COLE: I have no trade.

THE SHOWMAN: Where is your home?

KING COLE: All gone, a long time past.

THE SHOWMAN: Your children then?

KING COLE: All dead, sir, even the last.
I am a lonely man; no kith nor kin.

THE SHOWMAN: There is no joy in life when deaths begin,
I know it, I. How long is't since you ate?

KING COLE: It was so long ago that I forget.

THE SHOWMAN: The proverb says a man can always find
One sorrier than himself in state and mind.
'Fore George, it's true. Well, come, then, to the van.
Jane, can you find a meal for this poor man?

"Yes," said his wife. "Thank God, we still are able
To help a friend; come in, and sit to table."

"Come," said her man, "I'll help you up aboard,
I'll save your legs as far as Wallingford."

They climbed aboard and sat; the woman spread
Food for King Cole, and watched him as he fed.
Tears trickled down her cheeks and much she sighed.
"My son," she said, "like you, is wandering wide,
I know not where; a beggar in the street,
(For all I know) without a crust to eat.
He never could abide the circus life."

THE SHOWMAN: It was my fault, I always tell my wife
I put too great constraint upon his will;
Things would be changed if he were with us still.
I ought not to have forced him to the trade.

KING COLE: "A forced thing finds a vent," my father said;
And yet a quickening tells me that your son
Is not far from you now; for I am one
Who feels these things, like comfort in the heart.

The couple watched King Cole and shrank apart,
For brightness covered him with glittering.
"Tell me your present troubles," said the King,
"For you are worn. What sorrow makes you sad?"

THE SHOWMAN: Why, nothing, sir, except that times are bad,
Rain all the season through, and empty tents,
And nothing earned for stock or winter rents.
My wife there, ill, poor soul, from very grief,
And now no hope nor prospect of relief;
The season's done, and we're as we began.

Now one can bear one's troubles, being a man,
But what I cannot bear is loss of friends.

This troupe will scatter when the season ends:
My clown is going, and the Tricksey Three
Who juggle and do turns, have split with me;
And now, to-day, my wife's too ill to dance,
And all my music ask for an advance.
There must be poison in a man's distress
That makes him mad and people like him less.

Well, men are men. But what I cannot bear
Is my poor Bet, my piebald Talking Mare,
Gone curby in her hocks from standing up.
That's the last drop that overfills the cup.
My Bet's been like a Christian friend for years.

KING COLE: Now courage, friend, no good can come from tears.
I know a treatment for a curby hock
Good both for inward sprain or outward knock.
Here's the receipt; it's sure as flowers in spring;
A certain cure, the Ointment of the King.

That cures your mare; your troubles
Time will right;
A man's ill-fortune passes like the night.
Times are already mending at their worst;
Think of Spent Simmy when his roof-beam burst.
His ruined roof fell on him in a rain
Of hidden gold that built it up again.
So, courage, and believe God's providence.
Lo, here, the city shining like new pence,
To welcome you; the Prince is lodging there.
Lo, you, the banners flying like a fair.
Your circus will be crowded twenty deep.
This city is a field for you to reap,

For thousands must have come to see the
Prince,
And all are here, all wanting fun.
And since
The grass was green, all men have loved a show.
Success is here, so let your trouble go.

THE SHOWMAN: Well, blessings on your heart for speaking so;
It may be that the tide will turn at last.
But royal tours have crossed me in the past
And killed my show, and maybe will again.
One hopes for little after months of rain,
And the little that one hopes one does not get.

THE WIFE: Look, Will, the city gates with sentries set.

THE SHOWMAN: It looks to me as if the road were barred.

KING COLE: They are some soldiers of the bodyguard.
I hope, the heralds of your fortune's change.

"Now take this frowsy circus off the range,"
The soldiers at the city entrance cried;
"Keep clear the town, you cannot pass inside,
The Prince is here, with other things to do
Than stare at gangs of strollers such as you."

THE SHOWMAN: But I am billed to play here; and must play.

THE SOLDIERS: No must at all. You cannot play to-day,
Nor pitch your tents within the city bound.

THE SHOWMAN: Where can I, then?

THE SOLDIERS: Go, find some other ground.

A POLICEMAN: Pass through the city. You can pitch and play
One mile beyond it, after five to-day.

THE SHOWMAN: One mile beyond, what use is that to me?

A POLICEMAN: Those are the rules, here printed, you can see.

THE SHOWMAN: But let me see the Mayor, to make sure.

THE SOLDIERS: These are his printed orders, all secure.
Pass through or back, you must not linger here,
Blocking the road with all this circus gear.

Which will you do, then: back or pass along?

THE SHOWMAN: Pass.

THE SOLDIERS: Then away, and save your breath for song,
We cannot bother with your right and wrong.
George, guide these waggons through the
western gate.
Now, march, d'ye hear? and do not stop to bait
This side a mile; for that's the order.   March!

The Showman toppled like a broken arch.
The line-squall roared upon them with loud lips.

A green-lit strangeness followed, like eclipse

They passed within, but, when within, King Cole
Slipped from the van to head the leading team.
He breathed into his flute his very soul,
A noise like waters in a pebbly stream,
And straight the spirits that inhabit dream
Came round him, and the rain-squall roared its last
And bright the wind-vane shifted as it passed.

And in the rush of sun and glittering cloud
That followed on the storm, he led the way,
Fluting the sodden circus through the crowd
That trod the city streets in holiday.
And lo, a marvellous thing, the gouted clay,
Splashed on the waggons and the horses, glowed,
They shone like embers as they trod the road.
And round the tired horses came the Powers
That stir men's spirits, waking or asleep,
To thoughts like planets and to acts like flowers,
Out of the inner wisdom's beauty deep:
These led the horses, and, as marshalled sheep
Fronting a dog, in line, the people stared
At those bright waggons led by the bright-haired.

And, as they marched, the spirits sang, and all
The horses crested to the tune and stept
Like centaurs to a passionate festival
With shining throats that mantling criniers swept.
And all the hearts of all the watchers leapt
To see those horses passing and to hear
That song that came like blessing to the ear.

And, to the crowd, the circus artists seemed
Splendid, because the while that singing quired
Each artist was the part that he had dreamed
And glittered with the Power he desired,
Women and men, no longer wet or tired
From long despair, now shone like queens and kings,
There they were crowned with their imaginings.

And with them, walking by the vans, there came
The wild things from the woodland and the mead,
The red stag, with his tender-stepping dame,
Branched, and high-tongued and ever taking heed.
Nose-wrinkling rabbits nibbling at the weed,
The hares that box by moonlight on the hill,
The bright trout's death, the otter from the mill.

There, with his mask made virtuous, came the fox,
Talking of landscape while he thought of meat;
Blood-loving weasels, honey-harrying brocks,
Stoats, and the mice that build among the wheat,
Dormice, and moles with little hands for feet,
The water-rat that gnaws the yellow flag,
Toads from the stone and merrows from the quag.

And over them flew birds of every kind,
Whose way, or song, or speed, or beauty brings
Delight and understanding to the mind;

The bright-eyed, feathery, thready-leggéd things.
There they, too, sang amid a rush of wings,
With sweet, clear cries and gleams from wing and crest,
Blue, scarlet, white, gold plume and speckled breast.

And all the vans seemed grown with living leaves
And living flowers, the best September knows,
Moist poppies scarlet from the Hilcote sheaves,
Green-fingered bine that runs the barley-rows,
Pale candylips, and those intense blue blows
That trail the porches in the autumn dusk,
Tempting the noiseless moth to tongue their musk.

So, tired thus, so tended, and so sung,
They crossed the city through the marvelling crowd.
Maids with wide eyes from upper windows hung,
The children waved their toys and sang aloud.
But in his van the beaten showman bowed
His head upon his hands, and wept, not knowing
Aught of what passed except that wind was blowing.

All through the town the fluting led them on,
But near the western gate King Cole retired;
And, as he ceased, the vans no longer shone,
The bright procession dimmed like lamps expired;
Again with muddy vans and horses tired,
And artists cross and women out of luck,
The sodden circus plodded through the muck.

The crowd of following children loitered home;
Maids shut the windows lest more rain should come;
The circus left the streets of flowers and flags,
King Cole walked with it, huddling in his rags.
They reached the western gate and sought to pass.

"Take back this frowsy show to where it was,"
The sergeant of the gateway-sentry cried;
"You know quite well you cannot pass outside."

THE SHOWMAN: But we were told to pass here, by the guard.
THE SERGEANT: Here are the printed orders on the card.
No traffic, you can read.   Clear out.
THE SHOWMAN: But where?
THE SERGEANT: Where you're not kicked from, or there's room
to spare.
Go back and out of town the way you came.
THE SHOWMAN: I've just been sent from there.   Is this a game?
THE SERGEANT: You'll find it none, my son, if that's your tone.
THE SHOWMAN: You redcoats; ev'n your boots are not your
own.
THE SERGEANT: No, they're the Queen's; I represent the Queen.
THE SHOWMAN: Pipeclay your week's accounts, you red marine.
THE SERGEANT: Thank you, I will.   Now vanish.   Right-about.
THE SHOWMAN: Right, kick the circus in or kick it out,
But kick us, kick us hard, we've got no friends,
We've no Queen's boots or busbies on our ends;
We're poor, we like it, no one cares; besides
These dirty artists ought to have thick hides.
The dust, like us, is fit for boots to stamp,
None but Queen's redcoats are allowed to camp
In this free country.
A POLICEMAN: What's the trouble here?
THE SHOWMAN: A redcoat dog, in need of a thick ear.
THE POLICEMAN:The show turned back?   No, sergeant, let them
through.
They can't turn back, because the Prince is
due.
Best let them pass.
THE SERGEANT: Then pass; and read the rules
Another time.

THE SHOWMAN: You fat, red-coated fools.
THE POLICEMAN: Pass right along.

                              They passed. Beyond the town
A farmer gave them leave to settle down
In a green field beside the Oxford road.
There the spent horses ceased to drag the load;
The tent was pitched beneath a dropping sky,
The green-striped tent with all its gear awry.
The men drew close to grumble: in the van
The showman parted from the wandering man.
THE SHOWMAN: You see; denied a chance; denied bare bread.
KING COLE: I know the stony road that artists tread.
THE SHOWMAN: You take it very mildly, if you do
             How would you act if this were done to you?
KING COLE: Go to the Mayor.
THE SHOWMAN: I am not that kind,
             I'll kneel to no Court prop with painted rind.
             You and your snivelling to them may go hang.
             I say: "God curse the Prince and all his gang."
THE WIFE: Ah, no, my dear, for Life hurts everyone,
             Without our cursing. Let the poor Prince be;
             We artist folk are happier folk than he,
             Hard as it is.
THE SHOWMAN: I say: God let him see
             And taste and know this misery that he makes.
             He strains a poor man's spirit till it breaks,
             And then he hangs him, while a poor man's
             gift
             He leaves unhelped, to wither or to drift.
             Sergeants at city gates are all his care.
             We are but outcast artists in despair.
             They dress in scarlet and he gives them gold.
KING COLE: Trust still to Life, the day is not yet old.
THE SHOWMAN: By God! our lives are all we have to trust.

KING COLE: Life changes every day and ever must.

THE SHOWMAN: It has not changed with us, this season, yet.

KING COLE: Life is as just as Death; Life pays its debt.

THE SHOWMAN: What justice is there in our suffering so?

KING COLE: This: that not knowing, we should try to know.

THE SHOWMAN: Try. A sweet doctrine for a broken heart.

KING COLE: The best (men say) in every manly part.

THE SHOWMAN: Is it, by Heaven? I have tried it, I.
I tell you, friend, your justice is a lie;
Your comfort is a lie, your peace a fraud;
Your trust a folly and your cheer a gaud.
I know what men are, having gone these roads.
Poor bankrupt devils, sweating under loads
While others suck their blood and smile and
smile.
You be an artist on the roads a while,
You'll know what justice comes with suffering
then.

KING COLE: Friend, I am one grown old with sorrowing
men.

THE SHOWMAN: The old are tamed, they have not blood to feel.

KING COLE: They've blood to hurt, if not enough to heal.
I have seen sorrow close and suffering close.
I know their ways with men, if any knows.
I know the harshness of the way they have
To loose the base and prison up the brave.
I know that some have found the depth they
trod
In deepest sorrow is the heart of God.
Up on the bitter iron there is peace.

In the dark night of prison comes release,
In the black midnight still the cock will crow.
There is a help that the abandoned know
Deep in the heart, that conquerors cannot feel.

Abide in hope the turning of the wheel,
The luck will alter and the star will rise.

His presence seemed to change before their eyes.
The old, bent, ragged, glittering, wandering fellow,
With thready blood-streaks in the rided yellow
Of cheek and eye, seemed changed to one who held
Earth and the spirit like a king of eld.
He spoke again: "You have been kind," said he.
"In your own trouble you have thought of me.
God will repay. To him who gives is given,
Corn, water, wine, the world, the starry heaven."

Then, like a poor old man, he took his way
Back to the city, while the showman gazed
After his figure like a man amazed.

THE WIFE: I think that traveller was an angel sent.
THE SHOWMAN: A most strange man.   I wonder what he meant.
THE WIFE: Comfort was what he meant, in our distress.
THE SHOWMAN: No words of his can make our trouble less.
THE WIFE: O, Will, he made me feel the luck would change.
               Look at him, husband; there is something
               strange
               About him there; a robin redbreast comes
               Hopping about his feet as though for crumbs,
               And little long-tailed tits and wrens that sing
               Perching upon him.
THE SHOWMAN: What a wondrous thing!
               I've read of such, but never seen it.
THE WIFE: Look,
               These were the dishes and the food he took.
THE SHOWMAN: Yes: those were they.   What of it?
THE WIFE: Did he eat?

THE SHOWMAN: Yes; bread and cheese; he would not touch the
meat.
THE WIFE: But see, the cheese is whole, the loaf unbroken,
And both are fresh.   And see, another token:—
Those hard green apples that the farmer gave
Have grown to these gold globes, like Blen-
heims brave;
And look, how came these plums of Pershore
here?
THE SHOWMAN: We have been sitting with a saint, my dear.
THE WIFE.   Look at the butterflies!
                                        Like floating flowers
Came butterflies, the souls of summer hours,
Fluttering about the van; Red Admirals rich,
Scarlet and pale on breathing speeds of pitch,
Brimstones, like yellow poppy petals blown,
Brown ox-eyed Peacocks in their purpled roan,
Blue, silvered things that haunt the grassy chalk,
Green Hairstreaks bright as green shoots on a stalk,
And that dark prince, the oakwood haunting thing
Dyed with blue burnish like the mallard's wing.
"He was a saint of God," the showman cried.

Meanwhile, within the town, from man to man
The talk about the wondrous circus ran.
All were agreed, that nothing ever known
Had thrilled so tense the marrow in their bone.
All were agreed, that sights so beautiful
Made the Queen's court with all its soldiers dull,
Made all the red-wrapped masts and papered strings
Seem fruit of death, not lovely living things.
And some said loudly that though time were short,
Men still might hire the circus for the Court.
And some, agreeing, sought the Mayor's hall,
To press petition for the show's recall.

But as they neared the hall, behold, there came
A stranger to them dressed as though in flame;
An old, thin, grinning glitterer, decked with green,
With thready blood-streaks in his visage lean,
And at his wrinkled eyes a look of mirth
Not common among men who walk the earth;
Yet from his pocket poked a flute of wood,
And little birds were following him for food.

"Sirs," said King Cole (for it was he), "I know
You seek the Mayor, but you need not so;
I have this moment spoken with his grace.
He grants the circus warrant to take place
Within the city, should the Prince see fit
To watch such pastime; here is his permit.
I go this instant to the Prince to learn
His wish herein: wait here till I return."

They waited while the old man passed the sentry
Beside the door, and vanished through the entry.
They thought, "This old man shining like New Spain,
Must be the Prince's lordly chamberlain.
His cloth of gold so shone, it seemed to burn;
Wait till he comes." They stayed for his return.

Meanwhile, above, the Prince stood still to bide
The nightly mercy of the eventide,
Brought nearer by each hour that chimed and ceased.
His head was weary with the city feast
But newly risen from. He stood alone
As heavy as the day's foundation stone.

The room he stood in was an ancient hall.
Portraits of long dead men were on the wall.
From the dull crimson of their robes there stared

Passionless eyes, long dead, that judged and glared.
Above them were the oaken corbels set,
Of angels reaching hands that never met,
Where in the spring the swallows came to build.

It was the meeting chamber of the Guild.

From where he stood, the Prince could see a yard
Paved with old slabs and cobbles cracked and scarred
Where weeds had pushed, and tiles and broken glass
Had fallen and been trodden in the grass.
A gutter dripped upon it from the rain.

"It puts a crown of lead upon my brain
To live this life of princes," thought the Prince.
"To be a king is to be like a quince,
Bitter himself, yet flavour to the rest.
To be a cat among the hay were best;
There in the upper darkness of the loft,
With green eyes bright, soft-lying, purring soft,
Hearing the rain without; not forced, as I,
To lay foundation stones until I die,
Or sign State-papers till my hand is sick.
The man who plaits straw crowns upon a rick
Is happier in his crown than I the King.
And yet, this day, a very marvellous thing
Came by me as I walked the chamber here.
Once in my childhood, in my seventh year,
I saw them come, and now they have returned,
Those strangers, riding upon cars that burned,
Or seemed to burn, with gold, while music thrilled,
Then beauty following till my heart was filled,
And life seemed peopled from eternity.

They brought down Beauty and Wisdom from the sky
Into the streets, those strangers; I could see

Beauty and wisdom looking up at me
As then, in childhood, as they passed below.

Men would not let me know them long ago,
Those strangers bringing joy. They will not now.
I am a prince with gold about my brow;
Duty, not joy, is all a prince's share.

And yet, those strangers from I know not where,
From glittering lands, from unknown cities far
Beyond the sea-plunge of the evening star,
Would give me life, which princedom cannot give.
They would be revelation: I should live.
I may not deal with wisdom, being a king."

There came a noise of someone entering;
He turned his weary head to see who came.

It was King Cole, arrayed as though in flame,
Like a white opal, glowing from within,
He entered there in snowy cramoisin.
The Prince mistook him for a city lord,
He turned to him and waited for his word.

"Sir," said King Cole, "I come to bring you news.
Sir, in the weary life that princes use
There is scant time for any prince or king
To taste delights that artists have and bring.
But here, to-night, no other duty calls,
And circus artists are without the walls.
Will you not see them, sir?"

THE PRINCE: Who are these artists; do they paint or write?
KING COLE: No, but they serve the arts and love delight.
THE PRINCE: What can they do?

KING COLE: They know full many a rite
That holds the watcher spell-bound, and they
know
Gay plays of ghosts and jokes of long ago;
And beauty of bright speed their horses bring,
Ridden barebacked at gallop round the ring
By girls who stand upon the racing team.
Jugglers they have, of whom the children
dream,
Who pluck live rabbits from between their lips
And balance marbles on their finger-tips.
Will you not see them, sir? And then, they
dance.

"Ay," said the Prince, "and thankful for the chance.
So thankful, that these bags of gold shall buy
Leave for all comers to be glad as I.

And yet, I know not if the Court permits.
King's pleasures must be sifted through the wits
Or want of wit of many a courtly brain.
I get the less and chokings of the drain,
Not the bright rippling that I perish for."

KING COLE: Sir, I will open the forbidden door,
                Which, opened, they will enter all in haste.
                The life of man is stronger than good taste.
THE PRINCE: Custom is stronger than the life of man.
KING COLE: Custom is but a way that life began.
THE PRINCE: A withering way that makes the leafage fall,
                Custom, like Winter, is the King of all.
KING COLE: Winter makes water solid, yet the spring,
                That is but flowers, is a stronger thing.
                Custom, the ass man rides, will plod for years,
                But laughter kills him and he dies at tears.

One word of love, one spark from beauty's
fire,
And custom is a memory; listen, sire.

Then at a window looking on the street
He played his flute like leaves or snowflakes falling,
Till men and women, passing, thought: "How sweet;
These notes are in our hearts like flowers falling."
And then, they thought, "An unknown voice is calling
Like April calling to the seed in earth;
Madness is quickening deadness into birth."

And then, as in the spring when first men hear,
Beyond the black-twigged hedge, the lambling's cry
Coming across the snow, a note of cheer
Before the storm-cock tells that spring is nigh,
Before the first green bramble pushes shy,
And all the blood leaps at the lambling's notes,
The piping brought men's hearts into their throats.

Till all were stirred, however old and grand;
Generals bestarred, old statesmen, courtiers prim
(Whose lips kissed nothing but the Monarch's hand),
Stirred in their courtly minds recesses dim,
The sap of life stirred in the dreary limb.
The old eyes brightened o'er the pouncet-box,
Remembering loves, and brawls, and mains of cocks.

And through the town the liquid piping's gladness
Thrilled on its way, rejoicing all who heard,
To thrust aside their dullness or their sadness
And follow blithely as the fluting stirred
They hurried to the guild like horses spurred.
There in the road they mustered to await,
They knew not what, a dream, a joy, a fate.

And man to man in exaltation cried:
"Something has come to make us young again.
Wisdom has come, and Beauty, Wisdom's bride,
And youth like flowering April after rain."
But still the fluting piped and men were fain
To sing and ring the bells, they knew not why
Save that their hearts were in an ecstasy.

Then to the balcony above them came
King Cole the shining in his robe of flame;
Behind him came the Prince, who smiled and bowed.
King Cole made silence: then addressed the crowd.

"Friends, fellow mortals, bearers of the ghost
That burns, and breaks its lamp, but is not lost.
This day, for one brief hour, a key is given
To all, however poor, to enter heaven.
The Bringers Down of Beauty from the stars,
Have reached this city in their golden cars.
They ask, to bring you beauty, if you will.
You do not answer: rightly, you are still.
But you will come, to watch the image move
Of all you dreamed or had the strength to love.

Come to the Ring, the image of the path
That this our planet through the Heaven hath;
Behold man's skill, man's wisdom, man's delight,
And woman's beauty, imaged to the height.

Come, for our rulers come; and Death, whose feet
Tread at the door, permits a minute's sweet;
To each man's soul vouchsafes a glimpse, a gleam,
A touch, a breath of his intensest dream.
Now, to that glimpse, that moment, come with me;
Our rulers come.

O brother let there be
Such welcome to our Prince as never was.
Let there be flowers under foot, not grass,
Flowers and scented rushes and the sprays
Of purple bramble reddening into blaze.
Let there be bells rung backward till the tune
Be as the joy of all the bees in June.
Let float your flags, and let your lanterns rise
Like fruit upon the trees in Paradise,
In many-coloured lights as rich as Rome
O'er road and tent; and let the children come,
It is their world, these Beauty Dwellers bring."

Then, like the song of all the birds of spring
He played his flute, and all who heard it cried,
"Strew flowers before our rulers to the Ring."
The courtiers hurried for their coats of pride
The upturned faces in that market wide
Glowed in the sunset to a beauty grave
Such as the faces of immortals have.

And work was laid aside on desk and bench,
The red-lined ledger summed no penny more,
From lamp-blacked fingers the mechanic's wrench
Dropped to the kinking wheel chains on the floor,
The farmer shut the hen roost: at the store
The boys put up the shutters and ran hooting
Wild with delight in freedom to the fluting.

And now the fluting led that gathered tide
Of men and women forward through the town,
And flowers seemed to fall from every side,
White starry blossoms such as brooks bow down,
White petals clinging in the hair and gown;

And those who marched there thought that starry flowers
Grew at their sides, as though the streets were bowers.

And all, in marching, thought, "We go to see
Life, not the daily coil, but as it is
Lived in its beauty in eternity,
Above base aim, beyond our miseries;
Life that is speed and colour and bright bliss,
And beauty seen and strained for, and possest
Even as a star forever in the breast."

The fluting led them through the western gate,
From many a tossing torch their faces glowed,
Bright-eyed and ruddy-featured and elate;
They sang and scattered flowers upon the road,
Still in their hair the starry blossoms snowed;
They saw ahead the green-striped tent, their mark,
Lit now and busy in the gathering dark.

There at the vans and in the green-striped tent
The circus artists growled their discontent.
Close to the gate a lighted van there was;
The showman's wife thrust back its window glass.
And leaned her head without to see who came
To buy a ticket for the evening's game.

A roll of tickets and a plate of pence
(For change) lay by her as she leaned from thence.
She heard the crowd afar, but in her thought
She said: "That's in the city; it is nought.
They glorify the Queen."

                              Though sick at heart
She wore her spangles for her evening's part,
To dance upon the barebacked horse and sing.

Green velvet was her dress, with tinselling.
Her sad, worn face had all the nobleness
That lovely spirits gather from distress.

"No one to-night," she thought, "no one to-night."

Within the tent, a flare gave blowing light.
There, in their scarlet cart, the bandsmen tuned
Bugles that whinnied, flageolets that crooned
And strings that whined and grunted.

                                    Near the band
Piebald and magpie horses stood at hand
Nosing at grass beneath the green-striped dome
While men caressed them with the curry-comb.

The clowns, with whited, raddled faces, heaped
Old horse cloths round them to the chins; they peeped
Above the rugs; their cigarette ends' light
Showing black eyes, and scarlet smears and white.

They watched the empty benches, and the wry
Green curtain door which no one entered by.

Two little children entered and sat still
With bright wide-opened eyes that stared their fill,
And red lips round in wonder smeared with tints
From hands and handkerchiefs and peppermints.

A farm lad entered. That was all the house.

"Strike up the band to give the folk a rouse,"
The showman said, "They must be all outside."
He said it boldly, though he knew he lied.

Sad as a funeral march for pleasure gone
The band lamented out, "He's got them on."
Then paused, as usual, for the crowd to come.
Nobody came, though from without a hum
Of instruments and singing slowly rose.
"Free feast, with fireworks and public shows,"
The bandsmen growled, "An empty house again.
Two children and a ploughboy and the rain.
And then a night march through the mud," they said.

Now to the gate, King Cole his piping played.
The showman's wife from out her window peering
Saw, in the road, a crowd with lanterns nearing,
And, just below her perch, a man who shone
As though white flame were his caparison;
One upon whom the great-eyed hawk-moths tense
Settled with feathery feet and quivering sense,
Till the white, gleaming robe seemed stuck with eyes.

It was the grinning glitterer, white and wise,
King Cole, who said, "Madam, the Court is here,
The Court, the Prince, the Queen, all drawing near,
We here, the vanguard, set them on their way.
They come intent to see your circus play.
They ask that all who wish may enter free,
And in their princely hope that this may be
They send you these plump bags of minted gold."
He gave a sack that she could scarcely hold.
She dropped it trembling, muttering thanks, and then
She cried: "O master, I must tell the men."

She rushed out of her van: she reached the Ring;
Called to her husband, "Will, the Queen and King,
Here at the very gate to see the show!"

"Light some more flares," said Will, "to make a glow.
'God save the Queen,' there, bandsmen; lively, boys.
Come on, 'God save our gracious'; make a noise.
Here, John, bring on the piebalds to the centre,
We'll have the horses kneeling as they enter."
All sang, and rushed. Without, the trumpets blared.

Now children, carrying paper lanterns, made
A glowing alley to the circus door;
Then others scattered flowers to pave a floor,
Along the highway leading from the town.

Rust-spotted bracken green they scattered down,
Blue cornflowers and withering poppies red,
Gold charlock, thrift, the purple hardihead,
Harebells, the milfoil white, September clover,
And boughs that berry red when summer's over,
All autumn flowers, with yellow ears of wheat.

Then with bruised, burning gums that made all sweet,
Came censer-bearing pages, and then came
Bearers in white with cressets full of flame,
Whose red tongues made the shadows dance like devils.
Then the blithe flutes that pipe men to the revels
Thrilled to the marrow softly as men marched.
Then, tossing leopard-skins from crests that arched,
The horses of the kettle-drummers stept.
Then with a glitter of bright steel there swept
The guard of knights, each pennon-bearer bold
Girt in a crimson cloak with spangs of gold.
Then came the Sword and Mace, and then the four
Long silver trumpets thrilling to the core
Of people's hearts their sound. Then two by two,
Proud in caparisons of kingly blue,
Bitted with bars of gold, in silver shod,

Treading like kings, cream-coloured stallions trod,
Dragging the carriage with the Prince and Queen.
The Corporation, walking, closed the scene.
Then came the crowd in-surging like the wave
That closes up the gash the clipper clave.

Swift in the path their majesties would tread
The showman flung green baize and turkey red.
Within the tent, with bunting, ropes and bags
They made a Royal Box festooned with flags.
Even as the Queen arrived, the work was done,
The seven piebald horses kneeled like one,
The bandsmen blew their best, while, red as beet,
The showman bowed his rulers to their seat.

Then, through the door, came courtiers wigged and starred;
The crimson glitterers of the bodyguard;
The ladies of the Court, broad-browed and noble,
Lovely as evening stars o'er seas in trouble;
The aldermen, in furs, with golden chains,
Old cottagers in smocks from country lanes,
Shepherds half dumb from silence on the down,
And merchants with their households from the town,
And, in the front, two rows of eager-hearted
Children with shining eyes and red lips parted.

Even as the creeping waves that brim the pool
One following other filled the circus full.

The showman stood beside his trembling wife.
"Never," he said, "in all our travelling life
Has this old tent looked thus, the front seats full
With happy little children beautiful.
Then all this glorious Court, tier after tier!
O would our son, the wanderer, were here,
Then we'd die happy!"

               "Would he were!" said she.
"It was my preaching forced him to be free,"
The showman said.
               "Ah, no," his wife replied,
"The great world's glory and the young blood's pride,
Those forced him from us, never you, my dear."

"I would be different if we had him here
Again," the showman said; "but we must start.
But all this splendour takes away my heart,
I am not used to playing to the King."

"Look," said his wife, "the stranger, in the Ring."

There in the Ring, indeed, the stranger stood,
King Cole, the shining, with his flute of wood,
Waiting until the chattering Court was stilled.

Then from his wooden flute his piping thrilled,
Then all was tense, and then the leaping fluting
Clamoured as flowering clamours for the fruiting.
And round the ring came Dodo, the brown mare,
Pied like a tiger-moth; her bright shoes tare
The scattered petals, while the clown came after
Like life, a beauty chased by tragic laughter.
The showman entered in and cracked his whip.

Then followed fun and skill and horsemanship,
Marvellous all, for all were at their best.
Never had playing gone with such a zest
To those good jesters; never had the tent
So swiftly answered to their merriment
With cheers, the artist's help, the actor's life.
Then, at the end, the showman and his wife

Stood at the entrance listening to the cheers.
They were both happy to the brink of tears.

King Cole came close and whispered in their ears:
"There is a soldier here who says he knew
You, long ago, and asks to speak to you.
A sergeant in the guard, a handsome blade."
"Mother!" the sergeant said. "What, Jack!" she said,
"Our son come back! look, father, here's our son!"

"Bad pennies do come home to everyone,"
The sergeant said. "And if you'll have me home,
And both forgive me, I'll be glad to come."

"Why, son," the showman said, "the fault was ours."

Now a bright herald trod across the flowers
To bid the artists to the Queen and King,
Who thanked them for the joyful evening,
And shook each artist's hand with words of praise.
"Our happiest hour," they said, "for many days.
You must perform at Court at Christmas tide."

They left their box: men flung the curtains wide,
The horses kneeled like one as they withdrew.
They reached the curtained door and loitered through.
The audience, standing, sang "God save the Queen."
The hour of the showman's life had been.

Now once again a herald crossed the green
To tell the showman that a feast was laid,
A supper for the artists who had played
By the Queen's order, in a tent without.

In the bright moonlight at the gate the rout
Of courtiers, formed procession to be gone,

Orders were called, steel clinked, and jewels shone,
The watchers climbed the banks and took their stands.

The circus artists shook each others' hands,
Their quarrels were forgotten and forgiven,
Old friendships were restored and sinners shriven.
"We find we cannot part from Will," they said.

And while they talked the juggler took the maid
Molly, the singer, to the hawthorn glade
Behind the green-striped tent, and told his love,
A wild delight, beyond her hope, enough
Beyond her dream to brim her eyes with tears.

Now came a ringing cry to march; and cheers
Rose from the crowd; the bright procession fared
Back to the city while the trumpets blared.

So the night ended, and the Court retired.
Back to the town the swaying torches reeked,
Within the green-striped tent the lights expired,
The dew dript from the canvas where it leaked.
Dark, in the showman's van, a cricket creaked,
But, near the waggons, fire was glowing red
On happy faces where the feast was spread.

Gladly they supped, those artists of the show;
Then by the perfect moon, together timed,
They struck the green-striped tent and laid it low,
Even as the quarter before midnight chimed.
Then putting-to the piebald nags, they climbed
Into their vans and slowly stole away
Along Blown Hilcote on the Icknield Way.

And as the rumbling of the waggons died
By Aston Tirrold and the Moretons twain,

With axle-clatter in the countryside,
Lit by the moon and fragrant from the rain,
King Cole moved softly in the Ring again,
Where now the owls and he were left alone:
The night was loud with water upon stone.

He watched the night; then taking up his flute,
He breathed a piping of this life of ours,
The half-seen prize, the difficult pursuit,
The passionate lusts that shut us in their towers,
The love that helps us on, the fear that lowers,
The pride that makes us and the pride that mars,
The beauty and the truth that are our stars.
And man, the marvellous thing, that in the dark
Works with his little strength to make a light,
His wit that strikes, his hope that tends, a spark,
His sorrow of soul in toil, that brings delight,
His friends, who make salt sweet and blackness bright,
His birth and growth and change; and death the wise,
His peace, that puts a hand upon his eyes.

All these his pipings breathed of, until twelve
Struck on the belfry tower with tremblings numb
(Such as will shudder in the axe's helve
When the head strikes) to tell his hour was come.
Out of the living world of Christendom
He dimmed like mist till one could scarcely note
The robins nestling to his old grey coat.

Dimmer he grew, yet still a glimmering stayed
Like light on cobwebs, but it dimmed and died.
Then there was naught but moonlight in the glade,
Moonlight and water and an owl that cried.
Far overhead a rush of birds' wings sighed,

From migrants going south until the spring.
The night seemed fanned by an immortal wing.

But where the juggler trudged beside his love
Each felt a touching from beyond our ken,
From that bright kingdom where the souls who strove,
Live now forever, helping living men.
And as they kissed each other; even then
Their brows seemed blessed, as though a hand unseen
Had crowned their loves with never-withering green.

THE DREAM OF DANIEL

Weary with many thoughts I went to bed,
And lay for hours staring at the night,
Thinking of all the millions of the dead
Who used man's flesh, as I, and loved the light,
Yet died, for all their power and delight,
For all their love, and never came again,
Never, for all our crying, all our pain.

There, through the open windows at my side,
I saw the stars, and all the tossing wood,
And, in the moonlight, mothy owls that cried,
Floating along the covert for their food.
The night was as a spirit that did brood
Upon the dead, those multitudes of death
That had such colour once and now are breath.

"And all this beauty of the world," I thought,
"This glory given by God, this life that teems,
What can we know of them? for life is nought,
A few short hours of blindness, shot by gleams,
A few short days of mastery of dreams
After long years of effort, then an end,
Then dust on good and bad, on foe and friend."

So, weary with the little time allowed
To use the power that takes so long to learn,
I sorrowed as I lay; now low, now loud
Came music from an hautboy and zithern.
The house was dark, and yet a light did burn
There where they played, and in the wainscotting
The mice that love the dark were junketting.

So, what with sorrow and the noise that seemed
Like voices speaking from the night's dark heart
To tell her secret in a tongue undreamed,
I fell into a dream and walked apart
Into the night (I thought) into the swart,
Thin, lightless air in which the planet rides;
I trod on dark air upward with swift strides.

Though in my dream I gloried as I trod
Because I knew that I was striding there
Far from this trouble to the peace of God
Where all things glow and beauty is made bare.
A dawning seemed beginning everywhere,
And then I came into a grassy place,
Where beauty of bright heart has quiet face.

Lovely it was, and there a castle stood
Mighty and fair, with golden turrets bright,
Crowned with gold vanes that swung at the wind's mood
Full many a hundred feet up in the light.
The walls were all i'-carven with delight
Like stone become alive.   I entered in.
Smoke drifted by: I heard a violin.

And as I heard, it seemed, that long before
That music had crept ghostly to my hearing
Even as a ghost along the corridor
Beside dark panelled walls with portraits peering;
It crept into my brain, blessing and spearing
Out of the past, yet all I could recall
Was some dark room with firelight on the wall.

So, entering in, I crossed the mighty hall;
The volleying smoke from firewood blew about.
The wind-gusts stirred the hangings on the wall

So that the woven chivalry stood out
Wave-like and charging, putting all to rout
The evil things they fought with, men like beasts,
Wolf soldiers, tiger kings, hyena priests.

And, steadfast as though frozen, swords on hips,
Old armour stood at sentry with old spears
Clutched in steel gloves that glittered at the grips,
Yet housed the little mouse with pointed ears:
Old banners drooped above, frayed into tears
With age and moth that fret the soldier's glory.
I saw a swallow in the clerestory.

And always from their frames the eyes looked down
Of most intense souls painted in their joy,
Their great brows jewelled bright as by a crown
Of their own thoughts, that nothing can destroy,
Because pure thought is life without alloy,
Life's very essence from the flesh set free
A wonder and delight eternally.

And climbing up the stairs with arras hung,
I looked upon a court of old stones grey,
Where o'er a globe of gold a galleon swung
Creaking with age and showing the wind's way.
There, flattered to a smile, the barn cat lay
Tasting the sun with purrings drowsily
Sun-soaked, content, with drowsed green-slitted eye.

I did not know what power led me on
Save the all-living joy of what came next.
Down the dim passage, doors of glory shone,
Old panels glowed with many a carven text,
Old music came in strays, my mind was vext

With many a leaping thought; beyond each door
I thought to meet some friend, dead long before.

So on I went, and by my side, it seemed,
Paced a great bull, kept from me by a brook
Which lipped the grass about it as it streamed
Over the flagroots that the grayling shook;
Red-felled the bull was, and at times he took
Assayment of the red earth with his horn
And wreaked his rage upon the sod uptorn.

Yet when I looked was nothing but the arras
There at my side, with woven knights that glowed
In coloured silks the running stag to harass,
There was no stream, yet in my mind abode
The sense of both beside me as I strode,
And lovely faces leaned, and pictures came
Of water in a great sheet like a flame;

Water in terror like a great snow falling,
Like wool, like smoke, into a vast abysm,
With thunder of gods fighting and death calling
And gleaming sunbeams splitted by the prism
And cliffs that rose and eagles that took chrism
Even in the very seethe, and then a cave
Where at a fire I mocked me at the wave.

Mightily rose the cliffs; and mighty trees
Grew on them; and the caverns, channelled deep,
Cut through them like dark veins; and like the seas,
Roaring, the desperate water took its leap;
Yet dim within the cave, like sound in sleep,
Came the fall's voice; my flitting fire made
More truth to me than all the water said.

Yet when I looked, there was the arras only,
The passage stretching on, the pictured faces,
The violin below complaining lonely,
Creeping with sweetness in the minds' sad places,
And all my mind was trembling with the traces
Of long dead things, of beautiful sweet friends
Long since made one with that which never ends.

And as I went the wall seemed built of flowers,
Long, golden cups of tulips, with firm stems,
Warm-smelling, for the black bees' drunken hours;
Striped roses for princesses' diadems;
And butterflies there were like living gems,
Scarlet and black, blue damaskt, mottled, white,
Colour alive and happy, living light.

Then through a door I passed into a room
Where Daniel stood, as I had seen him erst,
In wisest age, in all its happiest bloom,
Deep in the red and black of books immerst.
I would have spoken to him had I durst,
But might not, I, in that bright chamber strange,
Where, even as I lookt, the walls did change.

For now the walls were as a toppling sea,
Green, with white crest, on which a ship emerging,
Strained, with her topsails whining wrinklingly,
Dark with the glittering sea fires of her surging,
And, now with thundering horses and men urging,
The walls were fields on which men rode in pride,
On horses that tossed firedust in their stride.

And now, the walls were harvest fields whose corn
Trembled beneath the wrinkling wind in waves
All golden ripe and ready to be shorn

By sickling sunburnt reapers singing staves,
And now, the walls were dark with wandering caves
That sometimes glowed with fire and sometimes burned
Where men on anvils fiery secrets learned.

And all these forms of thought, and myriads more,
Passed into books and into Daniel's hand,
So that he smiled at having such great store
All red and black as many as the sand,
Studded with crystals, clasped with many a band
Of hammered steel. I saw him standing there.
After I woke his pleasure filled the air.

THE WOMAN SPEAKS

This poem appeared to me in a dream one winter morning some years ago. In the dream, I was aware of a tall lady dressed for out-of-doors, with furs and a picture hat. I was aware, at the same time, of the whole of her past life, and of the fact that she was looking, for the first time, southwestwards upon Lincoln's Inn Fields, early on a calm, sunny Sunday morning. I saw the Fields as she did, in utter calm, sunny distinctness, as from the north-eastern pavement; the pigeons were picking food, the sun was shining, each brick and stone was distinct. I was aware of the fact that she had suddenly realised that life might be quite like this, and that were it so, it would be wonderful. At the same time, I was intensely aware of the whole of this poem, which explained her past, what she saw and what she felt. As she passed out of the dream, the whole of the poem appeared engraven in high relief on an oblong metal plate, from which I wrote it down.

> Bitter it is, indeed, in human Fate
> When Life's supreme temptation comes too late.
> I had a ten years' schooling, where I won
> Prizes for Headache and Caparison.
> I married well; I kept a husband warm
> With twenty general years of gentle charm.
> We wandered much, where'er our kind resort,
> But not till Sunday to the Inns of Court.
> So then imagine what a joy to see
> The town's grey vast and unappeased sea
> Suddenly still, and what a hell to learn
> Life might be quiet, could I but return.

THE RIDER AT THE GATE

A Windy night was blowing on Rome,
The cressets guttered on Cæsar's home,
The fish-boats, moored at the bridge, were breaking
The rush of the river to yellow foam.

The hinges whined to the shutters shaking,
When clip-clop-clep came a horse-hoofs raking
The stones of the road at Cæsar's gate;
The spear-butts jarred at the guard's awaking.
"Who goes there" said the guard at the gate.
"What is the news, that you ride so late?"
"News most pressing, that must be spoken
To Cæsar alone, and that cannot wait."

"The Cæsar sleeps; you must show a token
That the news suffice that he be awoken.
What is the news, and whence do you come?
For no light cause may his sleep be broken."

"Out of the dark of the sands I come,
From the dark of death, with news for Rome,
A word so fell that it must be uttered
Though it strike the soul of the Cæsar dumb."

Cæsar turned in his bed and muttered,
With a struggle for breath the lamp-flame guttered;
Calpurnia heard her husband moan:
                           "The house is falling,
The beaten men come into their own."

"Speak your word," said the guard at the gate;
"Yes, but bear it to Cæsar straight,
Say 'Your murderer's knives are honing,
Your killer's gang is lying in wait.'

"Out of the wind that is blowing and moaning,
Through the city palace and the country loaning,

I cry, 'For the world's sake, Cæsar, beware,
And take this warning as my atoning.

"'Beware of the Court, of the palace stair,
Of the downcast friend who speaks so fair,
Keep from the Senate, for Death is going
On many men's feet to meet you there.'

"I, who am dead, have ways of knowing
Of the crop of death that the quick are sowing.
I, who was Pompey, cry it aloud
From the dark of death, from the wind blowing.

"I, who was Pompey, once was proud,
Now I lie in the sand without a shroud;
I cry to Cæsar out of my pain,
'Cæsar, beware, your death is vowed.'"

The light grew grey on the window-pane,
The windcocks swung in a burst of rain,
The window of Cæsar flung unshuttered,
The horse-hoofs died into wind again.

Cæsar turned in his bed and muttered,
With a struggle for breath the lamp-flame guttered;
Calpurnia heard her husband moan:
                            "The house is falling,
The beaten men come into their own."

THE BUILDERS

Before the unseen cock had called the time,
  Those workers left their beds and stumbled out
Into the street, where dust lay white as lime
  Under the last star that keeps bats about.
Then blinking still from bed, they trod the street,
  The doors closed up and down; the traveller heard
Doors opened, closed, then silence, then men's feet
  Moving to toil, the men too drowsed for word.
The bean-field was a greyness as they passed,
  The darkness of the hedge was starred with flowers,
The moth, with wings like dead leaves, sucked his last,
  The triumphing cock cried out with all his powers;
His fire of crying made the twilight quick,
Then clink, clink, clink, men's trowels tapped the brick.

I saw the delicate man who built the tower
  Look from the turret at the ground below,
The granite column wavered like a flower,
  But stood in air whatever winds might blow.
Its roots were in the rock, its head stood proud,
  No earthly forest reared a head so high;
Sometimes the eagle came there, sometimes cloud,
  It was man's ultimate footstep to the sky.   ·
And in that peak the builder kept his treasure,
  Books with the symbols of his art, the signs
Of knowledge in excitement, skill in pleasure,
  The edge that cut, the rule that kept, the lines.
He who had seen his tower beneath the grass,
Rock in the earth, now smiled, because it was.

How many thousand men had done his will,
  Men who had hands, or arms, or strength to spend,

Or cunning with machines, or art, or skill,
  All had obeyed him, working to this end.
Hundreds in distant lands had given their share
  Of power, to deck it; on its every stone
Their oddity of pleasure was laid bare,
  Yet was the tower his offspring, his alone.
His inner eye had seen, his will had made it,
  All the opposing army of men's minds
Had bowed, had turned, had striven as he bade it,
  Each to his purpose in their myriad kinds.
Now it was done, and in the peak he stood
Seeing his work, and smiled to find it good.

It had been stone, earth's body, hidden deep,
  Lightless and shapeless, where it cooled and hardened,
Now it was as the banner on man's keep
  Or as the Apple in Eden where God gardened.
Lilies of stone ran round it, and like fires
  The tongues of crockets shot from it and paused,
Horsemen who raced were carven on't, the spires
  Were bright with gold; all this the builder caused.
And standing there, it seemed that all the hive
  Of human skill which now it had become,
Was stone no more, nor building, but alive,
  Trying to speak, this tower that was dumb,
Trying to speak, nay, speaking, soul to soul
With powers who are, to raven or control.

THE SETTING OF THE WINDCOCK

The dust lay white upon the chisel-marks,
    The beams still shewed the dimplings of the grain,
Above the chancel's gloom the crimson sparks
    Of Christ's blood, glowed upon the window-pane.
No brass or marble of a death was there,
    The painted angels on the wall whirled down
Trumpeting to man's spirit everywhere,
    The spire topped the bell-tower like a crown.
Now, on the tower-top, where the crockets ceased
    Like lace against the sky, they set at pause
The golden wind-vane, that from west to east
    Would turn his beak to tempests or to flaws.
It poised, it swang, it breasted the wind's stream,
The work was done, the hands had wrought the dream.

THE RACER

I saw the racer coming to the jump,
    Staring with fiery eyeballs as he rusht,
I heard the blood within his body thump,
    I saw him launch, I heard the toppings crusht.
And as he landed I beheld his soul
    Kindle, because, in front, he saw the Straight
With all its thousands roaring at the goal,
    He laughed, he took the moment for his mate.
Would that the passionate moods on which we ride
    Might kindle thus to oneness with the will;
Would we might see the end to which we stride,
    And feel, not strain in struggle, only thrill,
And laugh like him and know in all our nerves
Beauty, the spirit, scattering dust and turves.

FROM THE SONG OF ROLAND

Roland gripped his horn with might and main,
Put it to his mouth and blew a great strain;
The hills were high and the sound was very plain,
Thirty leagues thence they heard the strain,
Charles heard it, and all his train.
"Our men are fighting," said Charlemain,
And the Count Guenes answered him again,
"If another said that, we should think him insane."

                                      Ahoy.

Roland was broken by pain and outworn,
In great anguish he blew his horn;
Out of his mouth the bright blood did fall,
The temples of his brain were now all torn:
He blew a great noise as he held the horn.
Charles heard it in the pass forlorn,
Naimes heard it, the Franks listened all.
Then the King said, "I hear Roland's horn,
He would never blow it if he were not overborne."
Guenes answered, "You are old and outworn,
Such words are worthy of a child newborn,
There is no battle at all, neither won nor lorn,

                                       Ahoy.

"Moreover, you know of Roland's great pride,
It is a marvel that God lets him bide.
Without your command and knowing you would chide,
He took Noples and killed the men inside,
With his sword Durendal he smote them hip and side,
Then with water washed the fields where the blood had dried,
So that his killings might never be spied.

All day long he will horn a hare and ride,
Gabbing before his peers, showing his pride,
No man would dare attack him in all the world wide.
Press on your horse now.   Why do you abide?
France is still far from us over the divide."

Ahoy.

Count Roland's mouth bled from a vein,
Broken were the temples that held his brain,
He blew his horn with grief and in pain,
The Franks heard it and Charlemain.
The King said, "That horn blows a long strain."
Duke Naimes answered, "Roland is in pain.
There is a battle, by my hope of gain,
He here has betrayed him who did so feign;
Put on your war gear, cry your war-cry again,
Go and succour your noble train,
You hear clearly how Roland does complain."

Ahoy.

The Emperor made his trumpets blow clear,
The Franks mounted and put on their gear,
Hauberks and helmets and swords with gold gear,
Men had shields and many a strong spear,
And banners scarlet, white and blue in the air to rear.
On his war-horse mounted each peer,
And spurred right through the pass among the rocks sheer:
Each man said to his comrade dear,
"If we reach Roland ere he be dead on bier,
We will strike good blows with him and make the pagans fear."
But they had stayed too long, and they were nowhere near:

Ahoy.

THE HAUNTED

Here, in this darkened room of this old house,
   I sit beside the fire. I hear again
Within, the scutter where the mice carouse,
   Without, the gutter dropping with the rain.

Opposite, are black shelves of wormy books,
   To left, glazed cases, dusty with the same,
Behind, a wall, with rusty guns on hooks,
   To right, the fire, that chokes one panting flame.

Over the mantel, black as funeral cloth,
   A portrait hangs, a man, whose flesh the worm
Has mawed this hundred years, whose clothes the moth
   A century since, has channelled to a term.

I cannot see his face: I only know
He stares at me, that man of long ago.

  .   .   .   .

I light the candles in the long brass sticks,
   I see him now, a pale-eyed, simpering man,
Framed in carved wood, wherein the death-watch ticks,
   A most dead face: yet when the work began

That face, the pale puce coat, the simpering smile,
   The hands that hold a book, the eyes that gaze,
Moved to the touch of mind a little while.
   The painter sat in judgment on his ways:

The painter turned him to and from the light,
   Talked about art, or bade him lift his head,

Judged the lips' paleness and the temples' white,
    And now his work abides; the man is dead.

But is he dead? This dusty study drear
Creaks in its panels that the man is here.

        .   .   .   .

Here, beyond doubt, he lived, in that old day.
    "He was a Doctor here," the student thought.
Here, when the puce was new, that now is grey,
    That simpering man his daily practice wrought.

Here he let blood, prescribed the pill and drop,
    The leech, the diet; here his verdict given
Brought agonies of hoping to a stop,
    Here his condemned confessioners were shriven.

What is that book he holds, the key, too dim
    To read, to know; some little book he wrote,
Forgotten now, but still the key to him.
    He sacrificed his vision for his coat.

I see the man; a simpering mask that hid
A seeing mind that simpering men forbid.

        .   .   .   .

Those are his books no doubt, untoucht, undusted,
    Unread, since last he left them on the shelves,
Octavo sermons that the fox has rusted,
    Sides splitting off from brown decaying twelves.

This was his room, this darkness of old death,
    This coffin-room with lights like embrasures,
The place is poisonous with him; like a breath
    On glass, he stains the spirit; he endures.

Here is his name within the sermon book,
   And verse, "When hungry Worms my Body eat";
He leans across my shoulder as I look,
   He who is God or pasture to the wheat.

He who is Dead is still upon the soul
A check, an inhibition, a control.

   .   .   .   .

I draw the bolts. I am alone within.
   The moonlight through the coloured glass comes faint,
Mottling the passage wall like human skin,
   Pale with the breathings left of withered paint.

But others walk the empty house with me,
   There is no loneliness within these walls
No more than there is stillness in the sea
   Or silence in the eternal waterfalls.

There in the room, to right, they sit at feast;
   The dropping grey-beard with the cold blue eye,
The lad, his son, that should have been a priest,
   And he, the rake, who made his mother die.

And he, the gambling man, who staked the throw,
They look me through, they follow when I go.

   .   .   .   .

They follow with still footing down the hall,
   I know their souls, those fellow-tenants mine,
Their shadows dim those colours on the wall,
   They point my every gesture with a sign.

That grey-beard cast his aged servant forth
   After his forty years of service done,
The gambler supped up riches as the north
   Sups with his death the glories of the sun.

The lad betrayed his trust; the rake was he
  Who broke two women's hearts to ease his own:
They nudge each other as they look at me,
  Shadows, all four, and yet as hard as stone.

And there, he comes, that simpering man, who sold
His mind for coat of puce and penny gold.

.   .   .   .

O ruinous house, within whose corridors
  None but the wicked and the mad go free.
(On the dark stairs they wait, behind the doors
  They crouch, they watch, or creep to follow me.)

Deep in old blood your ominous bricks are red,
  Firm in old bones your walls' foundations stand,
With dead men's passions built upon the dead,
  With broken hearts for lime and oaths for sand.

Terrible house, whose horror I have built,
  Sin after sin, unseen, as sand that slips
Telling the time, till now the heapéd guilt
  Cries, and the planets circle to eclipse.

You only are the Daunter, you alone
Clutch, till I feel your ivy on the bone.

.   .   .   .   -

CAMPEACHY PICTURE

The sloop's sails glow in the sun; the far sky burns,
Over the palm tree tops wanders the dusk,
About the bows a chuckling ripple churns;
The land wind from the marshes smells of musk.
A star comes out; the moon is a pale husk;
Now, from the galley door, as supper nears,
Comes a sharp scent of meat and Spanish rusk
Fried in a pan.   Far aft, where the lamp blears,
A seaman in a red shirt eyes the sails and steers.

Soon he will sight that isle in the dim bay
Where his mates saunter by the camp-fire's glow;
Soon will the birds scream, scared, and the bucks bray,
At the rattle and splash as the anchor is let go;
A block will pipe, and the oars grunt as they row,
He will meet his friends beneath the shadowy trees,
The moon's orb like a large lamp hanging low
Will see him stretched by the red blaze at ease,
Telling of the Indian girls, of ships, and of the seas.

THE SHIP AND HER MAKERS

THE ORE

Before Man's labouring wisdom gave me birth
I had not even seen the light of day;
Down in the central darkness of the earth,
Crushed by the weight of continents I lay,
Ground by the weight to heat, not knowing then
The Air, the light, the noise, the world of men.

THE TREES

We grew on mountains where the glaciers cry,
Infinite sombre armies of us stood
Below the snow-peaks which defy the sky;
A song like the gods moaning filled our wood;
We knew no men—our life was to stand staunch,
Singing our song, against the avalanche.

THE HEMP AND FLAX

We were a million grasses on the hill,
A million herbs which bowed as the wind blew,
Trembling in every fibre, never still;
Out of the summer earth sweet life we drew.
Little blue-flowered grasses up the glen,
Glad of the sun, what did we know of men?

THE WORKERS

We tore the iron from the mountain's hold,
By blasting fires we smithied it to steel;
Out of the shapeless stone we learned to mould
The sweeping bow, the rectilinear keel;

We hewed the pine to plank, we split the fir,
We pulled the myriad flax to fashion her.

Out of a million lives our knowledge came,
A million subtle craftsmen forged the means;
Steam was our handmaid and our servant flame,
Water our strength, all bowed to our machines.
Out of the rock, the tree, the springing herb
We built this wandering beauty so superb.

THE SAILORS

We, who were born on earth and live by air,
Make this thing pass across the fatal floor,
The speechless sea; alone we commune there
Jesting with death, that ever open door.
Sun, moon and stars are signs by which we drive
This wind-blown iron like a thing alive.

THE SHIP

I march across great waters like a queen,
I whom so many wisdoms helped to make;
Over the uncruddled billows of seas green
I blanch the bubbled highway of my wake.
By me my wandering tenants clasp the hands,
And know the thoughts of men in other lands.

SONNETS

Once we were masters of the arts of men.
　Poetry, music, painting, building, all
Beautiful noble arts were ours then,
　Decking this England as for festival.

A son of England could not lift his head
　Then without knowing rapture of delight.
The English hedgerow rose of beauty shed
　Into all English hearts its red and white.

Our current coins bore then the sacred stamp
　Of style in the used thing.　In the world's tower
In space's darkness, England was a lamp.
　Her lovely brain beheld; her hand had power

In these two things alone, her spirit shows
Her Saint was then Saint George, her mark, a rose.

Builded in every village in the land,
　Cut in the lasting stonework, you will find
Marvellous relics that an English hand
　Left as the tokens of an English mind.

Their spires (rough stone translated) lift aloft,
　Their gargoyles grin, their bells, in belfries dark,
Still dole the time by hours to the croft,
　Columns still bear the towers and are stark.

Over all England beauty was like June
    Deep in men's spirits, when we made these things,
Nightingales, dew, the dogrose and the moon,
    Beauty of queens, authority of kings,

And faith of men, all merged, that centuries on
Eternal things should shine as then they shone.

I saw the work of all the world displayed,
    The thinkers of the theatres of earth
Sent, to be shown the utmost they had made,
    Much of it mad, much pleasant, some of worth.

But, worthiest of it all, this English man's
    Stood out supreme, as, in a paling sky,
When stars go out, the morning planet scans
    Our twilit world with an untroubled eye.

There the work stood for England, and made mute
    Our enemies who mocked us with decay;
There was a life's devotion come to fruit,
    Enduring beauty keeping death at bay.

Here is the work. Who, greater than his age,
Will use this work to consecrate the stage?

I cannot tell who will, but only know
    That faithful work was never yet forlorn.
The best abides, the lusts and fashions go,
    Time and the grasses cover over scorn.

By unexpected ways despaired-of things
    Come into being after hope has ceast.
Over our fainting shoulders there are wings,
    By unseen hands our harvest is increast.

Here in our darkness now the powers of light
   Stir us to change this land that we have filled
With squalor and with nightmare and with night,
   To Beauty's self; they summon to rebuild,

Rebuild in beauty on the burnt-out coals,
Not to the heart's desire, but the soul's.

    .   .   .   .

BEAUTY

When soul's companion fails,
When flesh (that neighed once) ails,
When body shortens sails,

O soul, break through the netting
Of failing and forgetting,
See clearer for sun-setting;

See clearer, and be cheerly,
See thou the image clearly,
Love thou the image dearly.

For out of love and seeing
Beauty herself has being,
  Beauty our queen;
Who with calm spirit guards us
  And with dear love rewards us
In courts forever green.